ReSharper Essentials

Make your Microsoft Visual Studio work smarter
with ReSharper

Łukasz Gąsior

[PACKT] PUBLISHING

BIRMINGHAM - MUMBAI

ReSharper Essentials

Copyright © 2014 Packt Publishing

First published: February 2014

Production Reference: 1130214

Published by Packt Publishing Ltd.
Livery Place
35 Livery Street
Birmingham B3 2PB, UK.

ISBN 978-1-84969-870-2

www.packtpub.com

Cover Image by Michal Jasej (milak6@wp.pl)

Credits

Author
Łukasz Gąsior

Reviewers
Maciej Aniserowicz

Piotr Owsiak

Jacek Spólnik

Acquisition Editors
Kartikey Pandey

Llewellyn Rozario

Content Development Editor
Rikshith Shetty

Technical Editors
Shubhangi H. Dhamgaye

Shweta S. Pant

Ritika Singh

Rohit Kumar Singh

Copy Editors
Kirti Pai

Stuti Srivastava

Project Coordinator
Aboli Ambardekar

Proofreader
Maria Gould

Indexer
Hemangini Bari

Graphics
Yuvraj Mannari

Production Coordinator
Shantanu Zagade

Cover Work
Shantanu Zagade

About the Author

Łukasz Gąsior is a programming enthusiast with several years of experience. A big fan of ReSharper and jQuery, he is primarily involved in projects related to web applications (ASP.NET and ASP.NET MVC). He enjoys trying his hand at different technologies, such as creating Android applications, just for the fun of it. He strongly believes that JavaScript can be mastered just like any other language.

If you would like to get in touch, he tweets at `@lukaszgasior` and blogs at `http://gasior.net.pl` and `http://codingtv.pl` (both blogs are in Polish).

I would like to dedicate this book to my wonderful wife, Magda, and my son, Michał, who have always been there to support me in all of my efforts. I would also like to thank Piotr Owsiak, who many years ago, showed me why using proper tools such as ReSharper is important!

About the Reviewers

Maciej Aniserowicz is a software developer from Poland. His main focus is Microsoft .NET. He's been implementing web and service applications for almost 10 years now. During this time, he tried to not only constantly improve his skills, but also find pleasure and joy in his everyday work by experimenting with "alternative" tools and frameworks and avoiding productivity and "fun-killers" such as TFS and SharePoint.

His main interests as a software developer in general are test-driven development and the Git source control system.

Maciej blogs about software development and a developer's life in general. His blog (written in Polish) can be found at `http://www.maciejaniserowicz.com`. You can also find him on Twitter (`@maniserowicz`).

He is trying to gain experience as a speaker by visiting Polish user groups and conferences. His other goal is to deliver quality internal training to companies that are willing to learn how to use Git (and source control in general) and test-driven development properly.

He's been a Microsoft MVP (Visual C# category) since 2008.

Maciej lives his everyday life with a beautiful wife, a lovely daughter, and a stupid cat. He enjoys listening to metal music while coding.

Piotr Owsiak is a web developer with nearly 10 years of experience in .NET. He spends most of his time working in C# and ASP.NET, focusing on craftsmanship and good practices.

Piotr first started using Resharper Version 3, and he got hooked on it immediately and became a strong advocate of Resharper and other JetBrains tools.

Apart from .NET, he also likes to keep up with the interesting things that go on outside the .NET community. He likes playing with more dynamic languages such as JavaScript and Python.

Lately, he's been working as a contractor for financial institutions.

I'd like to thank my dad, Jan Owsiak, for giving me the inspiration to follow in his footsteps and start playing with computers.

Jacek Spólnik is a software engineer with over five years of commercial experience. In the past, he has created the .NET Object Database, NDatabase. He has also created software solutions for big companies such as GM, Loreal, and Lockheed Martin. He now heads the software engineering team that works for a top tier investment bank. He is focused on learning new things and actively spending time with his son and daughter.

www.PacktPub.com

Support files, eBooks, discount offers and more

You might want to visit www.PacktPub.com for support files and downloads related to your book.

Did you know that Packt offers eBook versions of every book published, with PDF and ePub files available? You can upgrade to the eBook version at www.PacktPub.com and as a print book customer, you are entitled to a discount on the eBook copy. Get in touch with us at service@packtpub.com for more details.

At www.PacktPub.com, you can also read a collection of free technical articles, sign up for a range of free newsletters and receive exclusive discounts and offers on Packt books and eBooks.

http://PacktLib.PacktPub.com

Do you need instant solutions to your IT questions? PacktLib is Packt's online digital book library. Here, you can access, read and search across Packt's entire library of books.

Why Subscribe?

- Fully searchable across every book published by Packt
- Copy and paste, print and bookmark content
- On demand and accessible via web browser

Free Access for Packt account holders

If you have an account with Packt at www.PacktPub.com, you can use this to access PacktLib today and view nine entirely free books. Simply use your login credentials for immediate access.

Table of Contents

Preface

ReSharper adds an amazing set of features that make Visual Studio a much, much better IDE, making a developer's work easier. It's probably the best plugin for Visual Studio.

Throughout this book, we will explain all the features that help you write smarter code, find things quicker, and provide better quality code.

ReSharper Essentials shows you how ReSharper improves a developer's work.

What this book covers

Chapter 1, Getting Started with ReSharper, explains what ReSharper is, what versions are available, and how to get them.

Chapter 2, Write Smarter Code, describes the features that allow you to write code easier. You will learn about generating code, using templates, and the available refactoring mechanisms.

Chapter 3, Finding What You Need Quickly, shows you how you can use ReSharper to quickly find the required class, file, or anything you need in your project. It also describes tools that show code references and structure.

Chapter 4, Making Your Code Better, discusses tools that will improve your code. You will learn how to use code-quality analysis and eliminate errors and code smells.

Chapter 5, Extended Support for Web Developers, describes the features that help in writing web applications. It explains how ReSharper helps write ASP.NET (MVC), JavaScript, TypeScript, and HTML/CSS code.

Chapter 6, Unit Testing, shows you how ReSharper helps run unit tests and how you can use it with dotCover to analyze code coverage.

Chapter 7, Extending ReSharper, comes as a quick introduction to writing plugins for ReSharper. It quickly explains the ReSharper API, the built-in tools that help in writing plugins, and how you can create a simple plugin step-by-step.

Chapter 8, Tools for Architects, describes new tools that help analyze the project structure and check referenced assemblies.

Chapter 9, Code Analysis Beyond Visual Studio, describes new, free command-line tools to run code analysis beyond Visual Studio.

Chapter 10, Recommended Plugins, provides you with a description of five plugins recommended by the author.

Appendix, Keyboard Shortcuts, provides you with a list of the most useful shortcuts covered in this book.

What you need for this book

As ReSharper is a Visual Studio plugin, you need to have Visual Studio installed on your computer. Unfortunately, the free Express edition is not enough. The screenshots presented in this book come from Visual Studio 2013, but all the presented features will also work with older versions starting from 2005.

You will also need ReSharper, of course. You can use the free 30-day trial to learn the presented features. We will show you how to get it in *Chapter 1, Getting Started with ReSharper*.

Who this book is for

ReSharper Essentials is aimed at developers who work with Visual Studio and want to make their work more efficient. It is most useful for new ReSharper users, but those who are currently using it will also find many useful things to learn.

Conventions

In this book, you will find a number of styles of text that distinguish between different kinds of information. Here are some examples of these styles, and an explanation of their meaning.

Code words in text, folder names, and filenames are shown as follows: "As you can see, this class starts with `ActionHandler`, which contains the name that we used in the `Actions.xml` file."

A block of code is set as follows:

```
if (false = $value$)
{
$statement$
}
```

Any command-line input or output is written as follows:

```
dupFinder [OPTIONS] source
```

New terms and **important words** are shown in bold. Words that you see on the screen, in menus or dialog boxes for example, appear in the text like this: "From this screen you can click on **Install** to run the installation process, or click on **Advanced** to configure more settings."

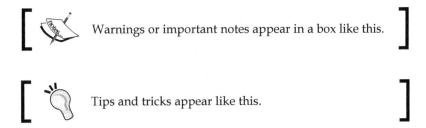

> Warnings or important notes appear in a box like this.

> Tips and tricks appear like this.

Reader feedback

Feedback from our readers is always welcome. Let us know what you think about this book—what you liked or may have disliked. Reader feedback is important for us to develop titles that you really get the most out of.

To send us general feedback, simply send an e-mail to feedback@packtpub.com, and mention the book title via the subject of your message.

If there is a topic that you have expertise in and you are interested in either writing or contributing to a book, see our author guide on www.packtpub.com/authors.

Customer support

Now that you are the proud owner of a Packt book, we have a number of things to help you to get the most from your purchase.

Errata

Although we have taken every care to ensure the accuracy of our content, mistakes do happen. If you find a mistake in one of our books — maybe a mistake in the text or the code — we would be grateful if you would report this to us. By doing so, you can save other readers from frustration and help us improve subsequent versions of this book. If you find any errata, please report them by visiting http://www.packtpub. com/submit-errata, selecting your book, clicking on the **errata submission form** link, and entering the details of your errata. Once your errata are verified, your submission will be accepted and the errata will be uploaded on our website, or added to any list of existing errata, under the Errata section of that title. Any existing errata can be viewed by selecting your title from http://www.packtpub.com/support.

Piracy

Piracy of copyright material on the Internet is an ongoing problem across all media. At Packt, we take the protection of our copyright and licenses very seriously. If you come across any illegal copies of our works, in any form, on the Internet, please provide us with the location address or website name immediately so that we can pursue a remedy.

Please contact us at copyright@packtpub.com with a link to the suspected pirated material.

We appreciate your help in protecting our authors, and our ability to bring you valuable content.

Questions

You can contact us at questions@packtpub.com if you are having a problem with any aspect of the book, and we will do our best to address it.

1
Getting Started with ReSharper

We, as developers, want to perform the right tasks using the right tools. For .NET developers, the most popular tool is Microsoft Visual Studio. It contains almost everything you need to create .NET applications. If it lacks something, ReSharper fills that gap and adds many more functionalities.

ReSharper, as a .NET developer productivity tool, helps you in the tasks you need to perform on a daily basis. It helps you avoid doing boring, repetitive and manual things. It makes refactoring your code easier, saves you time by supporting navigation through the project, and helps by generating code. In this chapter, we will cover the following topics:

- Introduction to ReSharper
- Downloading and installing ReSharper
- Basic configuration
- Integrating ReSharper with Visual Studio

Introduction to ReSharper

ReSharper is probably the best plugin for Visual Studio. It extends your favorite IDE with a lot of incredibly useful features.

ReSharper is developed by **JetBrains** (http://www.jetbrains.com). ReSharper v1.0 was released on July 21, 2004 as the second product of this company.

Thanks to the features, **code generation** and **code templates**, you will be able to write smarter code. **Navigation and search** will help you find things quicker. With **code analysis** and **code cleanup**, you can provide better quality software as ReSharper will find and highlight errors, potential problems, and bad practices in your code. ReSharper will support you with almost any kind of applications that you can write in Visual Studio.

Available versions

ReSharper comes in the following three versions:

- C# Edition
- VB.NET Edition
- Full Edition

These versions differ in support for the main language used in your projects. According to the name, if you are using C#, you should choose the C# Edition. If you are using VB.NET, you should choose the VB.NET Edition. Finally, if you are using both these languages, you should choose the Full Edition.

All other features, such as support for web development, unit tests, and XAML are the same in all of these versions except **decompiler**, which is not available in the VB.NET Edition.

Apart from the provided features, ReSharper can be categorized based on license. Depending on your needs, you can purchase any of the following licenses:

- **Commercial License**: ReSharper can be used by any developer in your company but the total number of concurrent users cannot exceed the number of purchased licenses
- **Personal License**: ReSharper can be used only by the person who purchased it

If you are a teacher, a trainer, a Microsoft's **MVP** (**Most Valuable Professional**), or if you are working on a non-commercial open source project, you can get ReSharper for free.

 For more information about ReSharper licenses, you can visit the **Licensing & Upgrade** page at http://www.jetbrains.com/resharper/buy/license-matrix.jsp.

Support for various versions of Visual Studio

ReSharper v8 provides support for Visual Studio 2013, 2012, 2010, 2008, and 2005. ReSharper works with all editions of Visual Studio except the Express Edition.

 ReSharper does not work with the Express Edition as it does not support add-ins and extensions.

It is also possible to use ReSharper with Visual Studio 2003. ReSharper 2.0 is still available; it provides support for this version of Visual Studio.

Support for various languages

ReSharper provides extensive support to many languages/technologies, which are listed as follows:

- C#, VB.NET
- ASP.NET, ASP.NET MVC, HTML, JavaScript, TypeScript, CSS
- NAnt, MSBuild
- XML
- XAML

It doesn't matter what kind of application you are working on, ReSharper will make your life easier!

Installing and configuring ReSharper

Although ReSharper comes in a couple of versions and supports various versions of Visual Studio, there is only one main installation package. The version used depends on the license key used during activation.

 During the free 30-day trial, you use ReSharper as a Full Edition by default. You can change this in the License Information window. To open it, navigate to **RESHARPER** | **Help** | **License Information...** from the Visual Studio toolbar.

Installing ReSharper

Installing ReSharper is quite straightforward. Perform the following steps:

1. Download the main installation package from the **Download ReSharper** page at `http://www.jetbrains.com/resharper/download/index.html`.

2. After opening the downloaded installation package, you should see the following screenshot:

In this step, you can select the versions of Visual Studio in which you would like to use ReSharper (in case you have more than one already installed).

From this screen, you can just click on **Install** to run the installation process, or click on **Advanced** to configure more settings.

3. If you have chosen **Advanced** settings, in the later steps you can choose what to do if you have a previous version of ReSharper already installed and how to change the installation location.

Configuring ReSharper

ReSharper is fully configurable. To access the ReSharper settings, you need to navigate to **RESHARPER | Options** from the Visual Studio toolbar.

Options

ReSharper configuration is divided into four areas, which are listed as follows:

- **Environment:** This allows you to change the general ReSharper settings such as UI and Visual Studio integration
- **Code Inspection:** This allows you to change the settings related to code analysis
- **Code Editing:** This allows you to change the formatting, naming, and code cleanup rules
- **Tools**: This allows you to change the ReSharper tool's settings, such as Unit Test frameworks, patterns used for to-do items, and navigation to external sources

 Code cleanup is a set of ReSharper features that make your code cleaner. Among the most important things, it can format your code, remove redundancies, and optimize the using (Imports in VB.NET) statements.

We will not go through all the available options in detail but present only those parts that, in our opinion, are the most useful.

Let's take a look at the tabs available under the **Environment** section.

The General tab

In this tab, you can change settings that are related to user interface. We suggest that you check the **Show managed memory usage in status bar** and **Show tips on startup** options. The first one will show you, on the bottom status bar, how much memory is used by ReSharper and the second one will try to teach you something new every time you open Visual Studio.

The Keyboard & Menus tab

This tab allows you to set how ReSharper integrates with Visual Studio. We propose that you check **Hide overridden Visual Studio menu items** and select **Visual Studio** as **ReSharper keyboard scheme**. The first one hides those options from the Visual Studio menu that are overridden by ReSharper; for example, the **Refactor** option in the context menu in the editor. This will indicate that you are using ReSharper features. The Visual Studio scheme adds shortcuts in order to avoid conflicts with the existing Visual Studio shortcuts.

In this book, we will present many shortcuts and all will be related to the Visual Studio scheme. For shortcuts from the **ReSharper 2.x/ Intellij IDEA** scheme, please check the ReSharper Documentation site at http://www.jetbrains.com/resharper/documentation/.

Now, let's look at the tabs that are available under the **Code Inspection** section.

The Settings tab

This tab contains general settings for code analysis. Our suggestion is to check all the options available below the **Enable code analysis** checkbox:

- **Color identifiers**
- **Highlight color usages**
- **Analyze errors in whole solution**
- **Show code inspection options in action list**
- **Show the "Import namespace" action using popup**

 Please note that checking the **Analyze errors in whole solution** option can hit Visual Studio's performance in big projects.

The Inspection Severity tab

This tab contains the most important settings related to code analysis. Settings are divided by language. It is highly recommended that you review these options to make sure that ReSharper will prompt suggestions that are consistent with your coding standards.

Next, we'll see the tabs under the **Code Editing** section.

The C#, VB.NET, and Naming Style tab

On this screen, you can find rules based on which ReSharper validates names used in your code. Same as with code analysis, it is recommended that you review the naming settings to make sure that they are consistent with your coding standards.

 There are many more interesting and useful settings. We encourage you to test a couple of different configurations to customize ReSharper to your needs.

Manage options

ReSharper v8 allows you to store configuration on the following three levels:

- **Computer**: This contains settings that are applied to all your projects.

- **Solution team-shared**: This contains settings for a specific project. These settings are stored in the `sln.DotSettings` file in your solution folder and override the settings specified at computer level. To share these settings with your team, you need to commit this file to your source control repository.

  Configuration on this level should be used to share common coding standards, such as naming conventions, code formatting, and code inspection rules, with your team.

- **Solution personal**: This contains your private settings. These settings are stored in the `sln.DotSettings.User` file in your solution folder and override Solution team-shared configuration. This file should not be committed to your source control repository as it will override other users' settings.

  Usually, this level is used to change environment options such as preferred shortcuts, IntelliSense behaviors, and ReSharper UI settings.

To open the **Manage Options...** window, navigate to **RESHARPER | Manage Options...** from the Visual Studio toolbar. You can also open this window by clicking on the **Manage...** button in the **Options** window.

Integration with Visual Studio

ReSharper is visible almost everywhere in Visual Studio. Sometimes, it is difficult to recognize if some option has come from Visual Studio or from ReSharper.

ReSharper extends Visual Studio in the following places:

- **Shortcuts**: Almost every ReSharper feature is accessible via a shortcut.

- **Custom windows**: ReSharper provides custom windows with more advanced features such as Unit Test Runner and Assembly Explorer. You can access these windows by navigating to the **RESHARPER | Windows** option from the Visual Studio toolbar.

- **IntelliSense**: ReSharper extends or replaces standard IntelliSense available in Visual Studio by providing more useful hints.

- **Code editor extensions**: In a visual way (for example, by icons), this shows you the available ReSharper options or marks the code on which you can run some ReSharper options.

As extending the code editor is the most commonly visible ReSharper feature, we will discuss it in more detail.

The following screenshot presents Visual Studio with some ReSharper extensions:

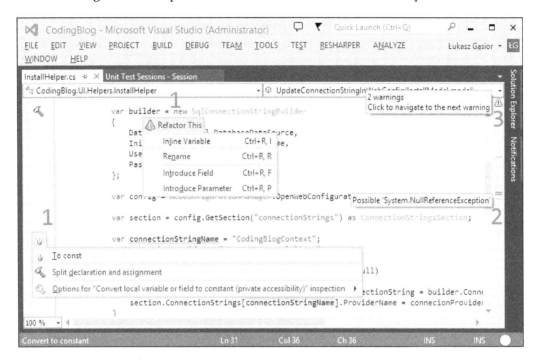

The most used features are accessible via context actions (numbered **1** in the preceding screenshot). Context actions are accessible by clicking on an icon or with the *Alt + Enter* shortcut. Context actions contain features related to code refactoring, code generation, navigation, and more. Quick fixes can be displayed along with context actions.

 Alt + Enter is your best friend in ReSharper. In a very smart way, it provides you with the needed options based on the context in which you are using this shortcut.

One of the most important ReSharper features is continuous code quality analysis. ReSharper highlights detected errors and warnings in the marker bar (numbered **2** in the preceding screenshot). The status indicator (numbered **3** in the preceding screenshot) is displayed on the top of the Marker Bar, which contains the summary of the found errors and warnings.

Summary

This chapter explained what ReSharper is and showed you how easy it is to start using it. You learned how to adjust the ReSharper configuration to suit your needs alongside your project and team standards.

In the next chapter, we will go deeper into the ReSharper features that will help you write code, and you will learn what it means to write smarter code.

2
Write Smarter Code

In this chapter, we will focus on one of the most important parts of a developer's work—writing code. ReSharper comes with many features that speed up writing and editing code. It is not possible to go through all of them in one book so we will focus on the most important ones.

We will cover the following topics in this chapter:

- Generating code
- Using code editing helpers
- Templates
- Refactoring

Code generation

There are many other ways to write code rather than simply pressing keys on your keyboard. ReSharper comes with many features that can generate code for you. You can find some of these features directly in Visual Studio but ReSharper comes with more. Even if ReSharper comes with some feature that exists in Visual Studio, ReSharper provides more user-friendly ways to use it.

Generating code for non-existent objects

Usually, when you are designing a class in your project, you start by writing complete code, such as class name, properties, and functions. When you are done, you can use that class in your application.

What if I told you there is a different way?

How about you start using your class before creating it and then let ReSharper create what you need?

This is a standard approach when you write applications using **Test Driven Design (TDD)**.

As the best way to learn something is to start doing it, we will show you how ReSharper helps with generating code.

Let's open Visual Studio and create a new **console application** project.

 To create a new console application project, navigate to **FILE | New Project...** from the Visual Studio toolbar. This will open a **New Project** window. Navigate to **Installed | Templates | Visual C# | Windows** from the left-hand menu and click on **Console Application** from the list of available projects.

By default, the console application project comes with one `Program.cs` file. Let's open it and write the following line inside the `Main(string[] args)` method:

```
new UserManager();
```

Your code should look like the following screenshot:

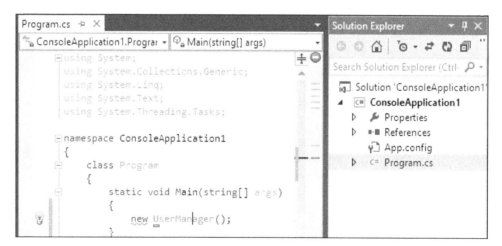

The preceding screenshot is a great example to show you the power of ReSharper. The name of our class, `UserManager`, is marked in red, which means that this class does not exist. This is also marked by a red line on the **marker bar**. The `new` keyword is underlined in blue to tell you that you are creating a new object without assigning it to any variable. The `args` parameter in the `Main` method and all `using` statements are grayed out to show you they are not used.

There are many problems that can cause an underlining of the code by ReSharper. To check what exactly is wrong, simply move your mouse cursor above the underlined word and ReSharper will display a pop up with a description of the problem that has occurred.

Finally, there is a context action icon, which tells you that there are some ReSharper actions that you can run on this code.

Before we continue, please have a look at the same code in the following screenshot, but without ReSharper:

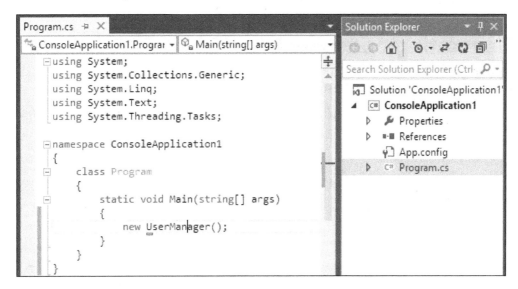

Without ReSharper, it looks like everything is fine with this code, doesn't it?

As you remember from the previous chapter, if there is a context action icon, you should press *Alt + Enter*. Then, select **Create class 'UserManager'** from the displayed options. This will create a new **internal** class, UserManager. To change this, move your cursor to the following line:

```
internal class UserManager
```

Press *Alt + Enter* and select **To public**. Now your new class is public.

In the same way, you can create methods, properties, enums, and everything you need. Just write the necessary code and press *Alt + Enter*!

Introduce variable

Now, let's come back to our first line. The `new` keyword is still underlined so we need to fix this. Move your cursor to the following line and press *Ctrl + R, V* (this means that you press *Ctrl* and *R* at the same time and then release *R* while still holding *Ctrl*, and then press *V*):

```
new UserManager();
```

This shortcut is associated with the **Introduce variable** feature and will convert your code to the following line:

```
var userManager = new UserManager();
```

Generating constructors

Now let's add a constructor to our class. In this constructor, we will assign a new value to the property `Repository`.

We do not have such a property yet, so let's create it inside the class. You can write the following code:

```
public UserRepository Repository { get; set; }
```

 Properties can be easily created using the **prop** snippet. Just write `prop` and double press *Tab*.

Now we are ready to create our constructor. Press *Alt + Insert* and from the newly displayed menu, select **Constructor**. This will open a new dialog window in which you can configure your constructor — you can select a constructor from a base class that you would like to implement. You can select the properties and variables that you would like to set in this constructor and change the access rights. A sample view of this screen is presented in the following screenshot:

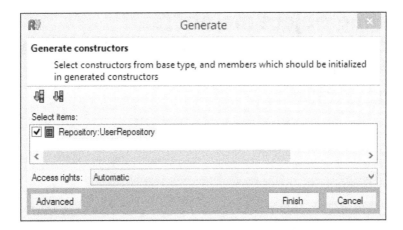

In our case, just check **Repository:UserRepository** and click on **Finish**.

As we created our constructor, ReSharper marked our first line because we are using their default constructor without parameters. By pressing *Alt + Enter*, you can generate a second constructor without parameters.

In your code, the `UserRepository` class is still marked in red—you already know what to do with this!

Surround with

Now, let's assume that we would like to assign a new value to our property only if the parameter in the constructor is not null. Move your cursor to the following line:

```
Repository = repository;
```

Press *Ctrl + E, U* and select `if` from the list. Now write your condition as shown in the following code:

```
if (repository != null)
```

 Surround with contains many more options. Check them and use them for your daily work.

Generating object members

So far, we have used *Alt* + *Insert* only to create the constructor but as you can see in the following screenshot, there are more interesting options:

```
public class UserManager
{
    public UserManager(UserRepository repository)
    {
        if (repository != null)
        {
            Repository = repository;
        }
    }

    public UserManager()
    {
        throw new NotImplementedException();
    }

    public UserRepository Repository { get; set;
}
```

Generate
- Constructor
- Read-only properties
- Properties
- Missing members
- Overriding members
- Delegating members
- Partial methods
- Equality members
- Equality comparer
- Formatting members

Let's describe those that are used the most:

- **Read-only properties** and **Properties**: These allow you to create properties for variables.

- **Missing members**: This is very useful when your class implements an interface or extends a class. This option allows you to create all members (methods, properties) that need to be implemented in your class.

- **Overriding members**: This allows you to override methods from inherited members. For example, you can use this option to override the ToString() method.

Using code editing helpers

Writing code is not only about writing, but also about getting more information on your code and support editing it.

Enhanced IntelliSense

IntelliSense is a standard tool in Visual Studio. ReSharper extends it by adding a couple of very useful features.

One of the most useful extensions for IntelliSense is **CamelHumps**, which allows you to filter options from IntelliSense by writing only capital letters from prompted options. By typing just UM (or um), ReSharper displays UserManager(), UnmanagedMarshal, and so on, as shown in the following screenshot:

```
static void Main(string[] args)
{
    new UM|
}                UserManager()
}                UnmanagedMarshal (in System.Reflection.Emit)
                 UnmanagedMemoryAccessor (in System.IO)
public cl        UnmanagedMemoryStream (in System.IO)
{
    publi        UpdateModificationStoredProcedureConfiguration<> (in System.Data.Entity.ModelConfiguration.Configuration)
    {            UrlMembershipCondition (in System.Security.Policy)
                 UmAlQuraCalendar (in System.Globalization)
                 STGMEDIUM (in System.Runtime.InteropServices.ComTypes)
                 ConventionUpdateModificationStoredProcedureConfiguration (in System.Data.Entity.ModelConfiguration.Configuration)

    }
```

ReSharper also extends the available options by adding objects from namespaces that are not used in the current file. In the preceding screenshot, only the first option comes from a developed project and the others come from unused namespaces.

For comparison, the options available when you are not using ReSharper are shown in the following screenshot:

```
static void Main(string[] args)
{
    new Use|
}                UserManager
}                UserRepository

public class UserManager
{
```

ReSharper provides **smart mode** too that, in a smart way, filters the available IntelliSense options. For example, if you are comparing enum values, it displays only enum members. If you are passing some parameters to a method, it will display only members with the correct type. Smart mode is made available using the *Ctrl + Alt + Space* bar shortcut.

The last extension that we would like to describe is providing IntelliSense for objects that don't exist. It sounds strange but the following screenshot explains what this means:

```
public void DoSomething()
{
    var myProvider = new MyProvider();
    myProvider.IsReady = true;

    if (myProvider.I)
    {                    IsReady    Field IsReady
```

As you can see, we have created a `MyProvider` class and a new `IsReady` property. After this, ReSharper knows that `MyProvider` will contain the `IsReady` property and display it in the available options.

Extending the code selection

It is very common that you will need to select some code. Normally, you select code by using the mouse or by using the *Shift* + arrows shortcut. ReSharper allows you to extend your selection by pressing *Ctrl* + *Alt* + the right arrow. Move your cursor to a word in your code and press *Ctrl* + *Alt* + the right arrow, which will select the whole word. Pressing *Ctrl* + *Alt* + the right arrow will extend the selection as shown in the following screenshot:

```
public UserManager(UserRepository repository)
public UserManager(UserRepository repository)
public UserManager(UserRepository repository)
public UserManager(UserRepository repository)
{
    if (repository != null)
    {
        Repository = repository;
    }
}
```

You can continue extending your selection until you select the whole file.

Safe delete

The **Safe delete** option allows you to check whether deleting an object member would break your code or not. The Safe delete option is made available using the *Alt* + *Delete* shortcut.

If it is safe to delete a selected member, ReSharper will just delete it. If not, ReSharper will display a warning or error for the conflicts found.

Auto-importing namespaces

As we have described previously, ReSharper marks objects that do not exist in red. However, this does not always mean that we would like to create it, because it can exist, but in namespace, which is not included in our file.

Such a situation is shown in the following screenshot:

```
public UserManager()
{
            System.Text.StringBuilder? (Alt+Enter)
    new StringBuilder();
}
```

In this case, you can just add the missed namespace by pressing *Alt + Enter*.

Quick documentation

ReSharper can provide you with more information about your code if you press *Ctrl + Shift + F1*. This will display a pop up similar to the following screenshot:

```
                                                    go to
public ActionResult Process(   public void
{                              UpdateConnectionStringInWebConfig
    var installer = new Inst   (InstallModel model)
    installer.UpdateConnecti     in class InstallHelper

                               Summary:
                               Updates connection string in web.config based on
                               values from InstallModel.

                               Parameters:
                               model: Contains data for creating connection
                                       string.
```

The **Summary** and **Parameters** description comes from a comment related to the `UpdateConnectionStringInWebConfig` method.

Templates

ReSharper provides you with a very powerful template mechanism that generates code for the most commonly used actions, such as creating a new class, constructor, and the `const` variables.

Templates as snippets

Visual Studio provides you with simple templates called **snippets** by default. ReSharper extends these templates with **Live Templates**. Live Templates can be accessed using the *Ctrl + E, L* shortcut or by using an associated name.

Do you need a GUID? Just write `nguid` and press *Tab*. Do you need an iterator? Write `iterindex`. Maybe you need to override the `Equals()` method? Write `equals`.

By pressing *Ctrl + E, L*, you can review all the available Live Templates.

File template

With Live Templates, you can generate some parts of code but ReSharper allows you to generate whole files too.

Creating a new file from a template can be done by pressing *Ctrl + Alt + Insert* in the code editor or by pressing *Alt + Insert* in the **Solution Explorer**.

Customization

Each ReSharper template can be configured. Also, you can add new templates if needed.

Templates can be managed through the **Templates Explorer** window. To access this window, navigate to **RESHARPER | Templates Explorer...** from the Visual Studio toolbar. A sample view of this **Templates Explorer** window is shown in the following screenshot:

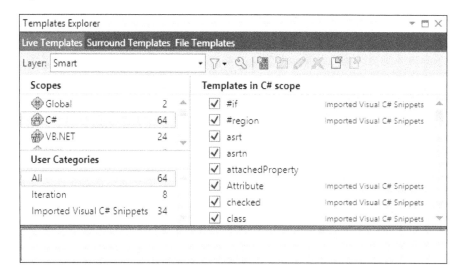

Separate tabs to manage **Live Templates**, **Surround Templates** (we have described them in the first part of this chapter), and **File Templates** are available.

To present how adding new templates work, let's do something useful and add a new Live Template for the unit test method. To do this, select **C#** in the **Scopes** area and click on the new template icon (third from left in the toolbar). This will open the template editor. Put `test` as your **Shortcut** name and the following code as your template body:

```
[Test]
public void $NAME$()
{
$END$
}
```

Let's look at the $NAME$ and END parameters. END is a built-in parameter and means a place in your code where the cursor will be placed. $NAME$ is our custom parameter and we need to configure it. You can do this by clicking on the **Choose macro** link below the **NAME** parameter and selecting **Constant value**. After this, a new textbox will be displayed that allows you to put the default value for this parameter. Let's put a `test` word there. Save your template and try it. In the same way, you can add Surround and File templates.

Multifile templates

ReSharper v8 comes with a new feature that allows you to create many files from one template.

How can this be useful?

Let's say that you often create a class and test this class at the same time. For now, you are probably creating two files in two steps. Why not do this in one step? Or maybe, according to your architecture, you need to create a couple of files to add new application modules, such as `UserRepository`, `UserManager`, and `UserSomething`. With ReSharper, you can create all these files in one step.

By default, ReSharper does not provide any multifile templates. You can add your custom template in the **File Templates** tab in the **Templates Explorer** window. Start by adding the standard file template. In the file template editor, there are two additional buttons available: **Add new file** and **Add file from existing template**, which allow you to add more files to your template.

A sample view of a template with two files is shown in the following screenshot:

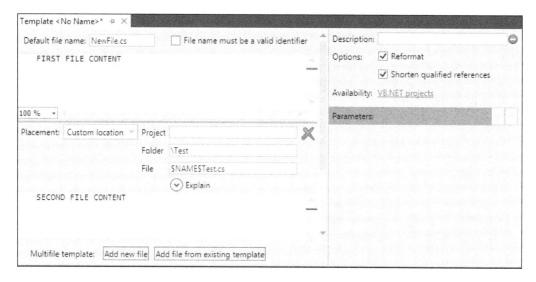

As you can see, you can specify a different destination folder and even a different project for different files.

Refactoring

You will seldom work with the ideal code. Almost every code can be improved – variables or methods can have better names, and code can be better structured and less complicated. This means that you would like to refactor such code. Refactoring code is a very hard and complicated process but ReSharper makes it a bit less painful.

Let's go back to our code that was used at the beginning of this chapter and refactor it a bit.

Rename

Let's say that we would like to rename the Repository property to UserRepository. Move your cursor to the definition or usage of this property and press *Ctrl + R, R*, input a new name, and press *Enter*. ReSharper will rename all occurrences of this property.

ReSharper also checks your string values, comments, JavaScript code, and other string literals as there can be some values related to our code that should also be updated. As you can see in the following screenshot, ReSharper displays all the places that can be potentially updated and allows you to check what all should be updated:

 When renaming a class name, ReSharper will also change the name of the file that this class contains.

Moving to a separate file

Now it is time to clean up our project's structure. We have three classes: `Program`, `UserManager`, and `UserRepository`, and all are in the same file. This is not a good practice, so let's change this.

Move your cursor to the class named `UserManager` and press *Ctrl + R, O*. From the displayed menu, select **Move To Folder**. This will open a new window in which you can change some settings related to moving your class. Let's put in a new folder named `Code`. In the **Target folder** field, write `ConsoleApplication1\Code` and click on **Create this folder**. Next, select **Put classes into separate files** and **Fix namespaces**. Finally, select the classes that you would like to move, `UserManager` and `UserRepository` in our case, and press *Enter*.

Quick, easy, and very useful.

There are two more options available after using the *Ctrl + R, O* shortcut:

- **Move To Another File**: This moves your class to a separate file in the same folder that the current file is located in

- **Move Type To Another Namespace**: This moves your class to a new namespace but it is still in the same file

Refactor this...

Rename and **move to separate file** are the two most used refactorings. More options are available through the *Ctrl + Shift + R* shortcut.

Let's move your cursor again to the name of the UserManager class, press *Ctrl + Shift + R,* and select **Extract Superclass**. This will allow you to create a base class for your UserManager class. In the new window, write the name of base class that you would like to create, select the members that should be moved to the new class, and press *Enter*.

If, instead of the base class, you would prefer to create the interface, just select the **Extract Interface** option.

Another very useful option is **Extract Method**. It is available after selecting the code that you would like to move to a new method. A sample window to extract the method is shown in the following screenshot:

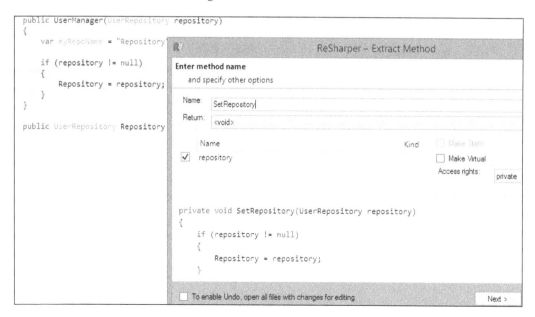

ReSharper comes with many other refactoring options. Every time you would like to refactor some code, press *Ctrl + Shift + R* and check if there is an option that can help you. You can find options such as **Convert Abstract Class to Interface, Convert Property to Method, Extract Class, Introduce Variable**, and many more.

Summary

It has been an interesting journey. We have learned about a lot of features that help you in writing code. Review this chapter, note down the presented shortcuts, and try to use them. If you are writing similar code again, maybe it is worth creating a custom template. Think how you can use the features presented in this chapter for your daily work. Write code smarter.

In the next chapter, we will check how ReSharper can improve navigation through our solution and makes it easier to find what you need. See you on the next page!

3
Finding What You Need Quickly

It is always important to find proper things quickly. ReSharper comes with many features to find files, code references, or navigate through your code quickly. Now let us find out how to use these features.

In this chapter, we will cover the following topics:

- Finding a proper file
- Searching for code references
- Navigating to library code
- Displaying the code structure

Finding files

In every project, code is divided into files. Depending on the size of your application, there can be hundreds or even thousands of files. More files make it harder to find the right one. ReSharper provides you with a few features that can help you find the file you need, quicker.

Every time you search for something in ReSharper, you can use the following **wildcards**:

- * (asterisk) as zero or more characters
- ? (question mark) as one character or zero characters
- + (plus) as one or more characters

CamelHumps are also supported by ReSharper and you can specify the line to which you would like to go.

Going to a proper file

The easiest way to find a file is to search it by its name. With ReSharper, it is very easy—just press *Ctrl + Shift + T* (**Go to File**) and write the name of the file that you would like to open.

Another useful way to open the proper file is to find a type contained in it. The type can be class, enum, and so on. Let's press *Ctrl + T, T* (**Go to Type**) and type the name of your class or any other type that you need.

Even if your project contains thousands of files, you are usually working on only a couple of them. In this case, it can be helpful for you to display a list of **Recent Files**. Just press *Ctrl + ,* and you will see a list similar to the following screenshot:

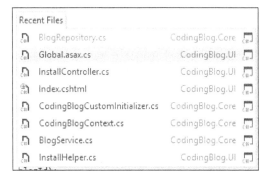

 You can easily filter a list of these files. Just start typing what you need!

Another often-used shortcut is *Shift + Alt + L*. It selects the currently opened file in **Solution Explorer**. It is useful when you need to open the current file properties or just open a file in the same folder.

Bookmarks

Bookmarks allow you to mark the most important places in your code and quickly navigate to them.

You can add up to 10 numbered bookmarks and unlimited non-numbered bookmarks. To create a numbered bookmark, just press *Ctrl + Shift +* any number from the keypad. With the same shortcut, you can remove the bookmark—just press it a second time on the same line. To go to a numbered bookmark, press *Ctrl +* that number.

You can also display a list of all bookmarks using the *Ctrl +* ` shortcut. The same shortcut allows you to manage non-numbered bookmarks.

The following screenshot presents a list of created bookmarks and markers with numbered bookmarks:

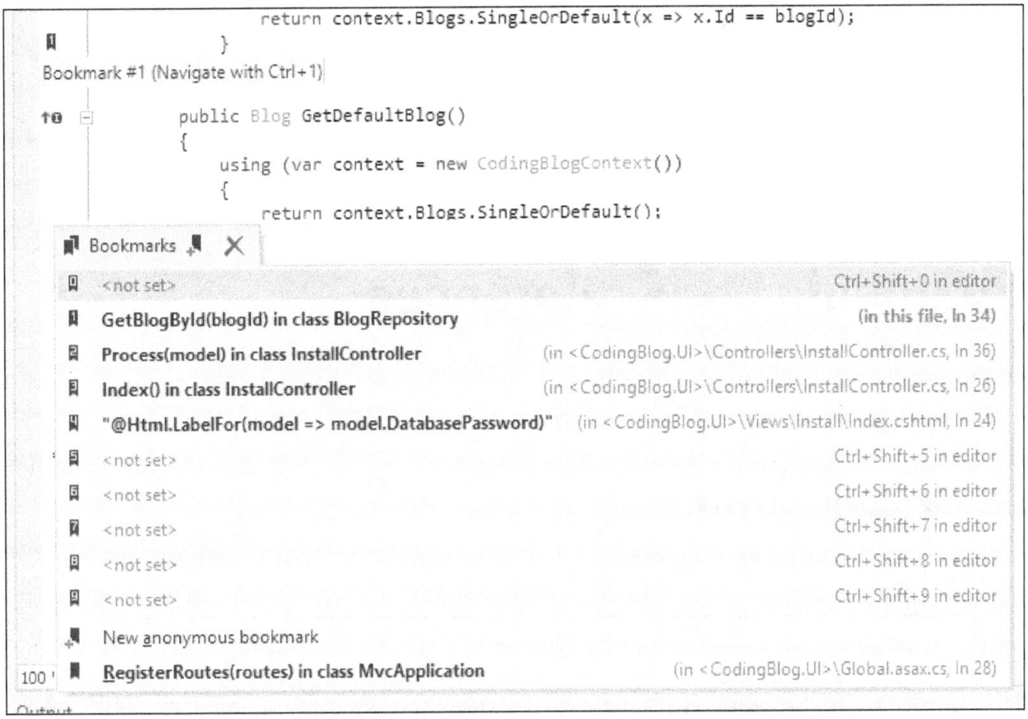

The last edited location

Additionally, to move between bookmarks, you can easily jump to the latest place at which you edited the code. To do this, press *Ctrl + Shift + Backspace*.

Go to Everything

As you can see, ReSharper allows you to find the proper file by searching for it using the name or type contained in it. To do this, you need to use different shortcuts, but not if you are using ReSharper v8.

ReSharper v8 comes with a new way to find files—**Go to Everything**. This is a merged version to search by name or type and really allows you to search everything! You can search almost everything you have in your code by your class name, method, and properties.

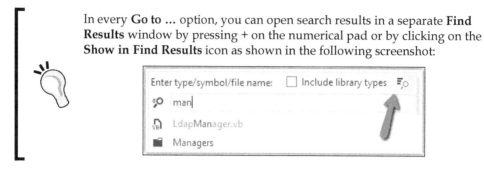

In every **Go to ...** option, you can open search results in a separate **Find Results** window by pressing + on the numerical pad or by clicking on the **Show in Find Results** icon as shown in the following screenshot:

To use the Go to Everything feature, just press *Ctrl + T*.

Searching code references

When we are writing about finding something in your project, it is not only about opening the files that you are working on, but also about finding relations within your code.

Go to Declaration

When you are analyzing your code, it is a very common scenario that you need to go to a particular place where a type is declared.

With ReSharper, you can do this by pressing *F12* (**Go to Declaration**) on your type, method, or property use/call. Another way to achieve this is by pressing *Ctrl*, moving your mouse cursor above a symbol, and clicking on the left mouse button.

Code usage

As you need to go to declaration, you probably also want to check where your symbol (class, method, and so on) is used. To do this, just move cursor to your symbol and press *Shift + F12* (**Find usages**). If there is only a single instance of the symbol being used, then ReSharper will just move you there. If there are more instances, then ReSharper will display a new **Find Results** window with all occurrences, as shown in the following screenshot:

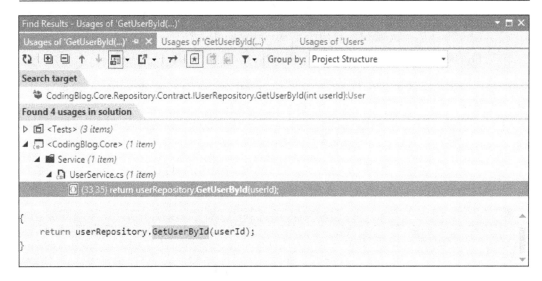

The **Find Results** window also allows you to display a preview of the code in which your symbol is used.

ReSharper can also highlight symbol usage in the current file. This will increase the readability of your code. The sample code with the highlighted userId variable is shown in the following screenshot:

```
public User GetUserById(int userId)
{
    using (var context = new CodingBlogContext())
    {
        return context.Users.SingleOrDefault(x => x.Id == userId);
    }
}
```

The Navigate to feature

The Go to Declaration and Find usages are two of the most used options when analyzing code references, but they are not the only ones.

You can find more options in the **Navigate to** feature (*Alt + `*). The more important ones that you will find there are listed as follows:

- **Go to Implementation**: This option is useful when your class inherits from another class or implements an interface
- **Extension methods**: This option displays all the available extension methods available for your type

- **Type of Symbol**: This option allows you to go to a type that your symbol has (that is, the type that is returned by your method)

- **Derived Symbols**: This option displays all the derived symbols

ReSharper can also visually indicate when a method overrides or implements another one, as shown in the following screenshot:

```
   6  ☐namespace CodingBlog.Core.Repository
   7   {
   8  ☐     internal class UserRepository : IUserRepository
   9   {
↑● 10  ☐         public User CreateUser(User userToBeCreated)
Implements method from interface 'CodingBlog.Core.Repository.Contract.IUserRepository'(click to navigate)
  12                using (var context = new CodingBlogContext())
```

Displaying code structure

So far, we have learned how to search for files and relations in your project. Now, let's see how ReSharper can help you view your code structure.

File members

When you are working with a file, ReSharper makes it very easy to navigate between different members in the file.

Simply press *Alt + * (File members) and ReSharper will display a list of all the available members, and will allow you to quickly jump to the selected member by pressing *Enter*.

The File Structure window

Additionally, you can display the file structure in a separate window. You can open the **File Structure** window by navigating to **RESHARPER | Windows | File Structure** from the **Visual Studio** toolbar or by using the *Ctrl + Alt + F* shortcut.

A sample view of the **File Structure** window is shown in the following screenshot:

```
File Structure - UserRepository.cs                      ▾ ⊄ ×
⊞ ⊟ ↑ ↓ ⊡▾  ⊧ ⊡ ⊴
☐ ⚙ UserRepository (in CodingBlog.Core.Repository)
      ● ↑● CreateUser(User userToBeCreated):User
      ● ↑● GetUserById(int userId):User
      ● ↑● EmailIsInUse(string email):bool
      ● ↑● GetUserByEmailAndPassword(string email, string password):User
```

Value Origin and Destination

With ReSharper, you can easily check how values are passed around in your code. By pressing *Ctrl + Shift + Alt + A* (Value Origin and Destination), you can open a menu with the following two options:

- **Value Origin**: This shows you where the analyzed variable comes from
- **Value Destination**: This shows you where the analyzed variable will be passed to

Results are displayed in the **Inspection Results** window. A sample view of this window is shown in the following screenshot:

In the previous screenshot, we analyzed the `blogToCreate` variable inside the `CreateBlog` method from the `BlogRepository` class. As you can see, this value can be passed from the `BlogService` or `BlogRepositoryTests` class. You can check how this value is passed to these classes or how it is created inside them. ReSharper displays the code preview, which shows you exactly how this variable has been used. You can easily navigate between these places, which makes the process of analyzing your code much easier.

Navigating to the library code

So far we have analyzed references between code only inside your own projects. How about analyzing the code of external libraries even if you do not have their source code?

Move your cursor to any method from the external library and press *Alt +* ` (Navigate to). From the displayed list, select the **Sources from Symbol Files** option. This option will try to display the code of the selected method based on debug information files (PDB).

If you do not have a PDB file, you can select the **Decompiled Sources** option.

The following screenshot presents the decompiled `Asserts.cs` file from **NUnit**:

As you can see, in code decompiled this way, you can use all the features described in this chapter.

By default, ReSharper will not decompile methods and will only display the method declaration. To enable decompiling methods, you need to navigate to **RESHARPER | Options** from the **Visual Studio** toolbar and then navigate to **Tools | External Sources** from the **ReSharper Options** window and check **Decompile methods**.

Summary

In this chapter, we saw an overview of the features that will help you find and navigate to a proper place in your code. ReSharper helps you with not only opening the necessary files, but also with finding relations and displaying your code structure.

Let's try to use these features the next time you open Visual Studio. And remember bookmarks — they are very useful!

In the next chapter, we will learn how ReSharper can help make your code better.

4
Making Your Code Better

So far, we have learned how ReSharper can help you write code and improve navigation around your project. In this chapter, we will focus on one of the most notable ReSharper features — code analysis.

In this chapter, we will cover the following topics:

- Code quality analysis
- Eliminating errors and code smells

Code quality analysis

The fact that you can compile your code does not mean your code is good. It does not even mean it will work. There are many things that can easily break your code. A good example is an unhandled `NullReferenceException`. You will be able to compile your code and you will be able to run your application, but there will be a problem.

ReSharper v8 comes with more than 1400 code analysis rules and more than 700 quick fixes, which allow you to fix detected problems. What is really cool is that ReSharper provides you with code inspection rules for all supported languages. This means that ReSharper not only improves your C# or VB.NET code, but also HTML, JavaScript, CSS, XAML, XML, ASP.NET, ASP.NET MVC, and TypeScript.

Apart from finding possible errors, code quality analysis rules can also improve the readability of your code. ReSharper can detect code that is unused and mark it as grayed, which prompts you that maybe you should use auto properties or objects and collection initializers, or use the `var` keyword instead of an explicit type name.

ReSharper provides you with five severity levels for rules and allows you to configure them according to your preference. Code inspection rules can be configured in the ReSharper's **Options** window. A sample view of code inspection rules with the list of available severity levels is shown in the following screenshot:

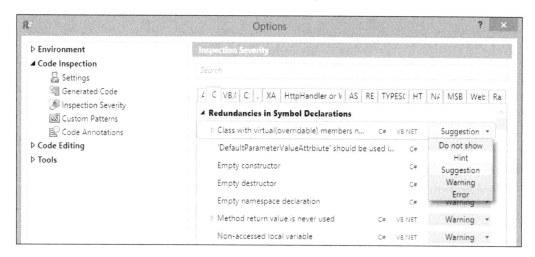

Background analysis

One of the best features in terms of code quality in ReSharper is Background analysis. This means that all the rules are checked as you are writing your code. You do not need to compile your project to see the results of the analysis. ReSharper will display appropriate messages in real time.

Solution-wide inspections

By default, the described rules are checked locally, which means that they should be checked in the current class. Because of this, ReSharper can mark some code as unused if it is used only locally; for example, there can be any unused private method or some part of code inside your method.

These two cases are shown in the following screenshot:

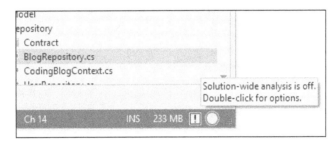

```
private User ValidateUser(string email, string password)
{
    var userR   Method 'ValidateUser' is never used   ();

    if (userRepository == null)
    {
        Expression is always false

    }

    return userRepository.GetUserByEmailAndPassword(email, passw
}
```

Additionally, for *local analysis*, ReSharper can check some rules in your entire project. To do this, you need to enable Solution-wide inspections. The easiest way to enable Solution-wide inspections is to double-click the circle icon in the bottom-right corner of Visual Studio, as seen in the following screenshot:

```
odel
epository
  Contract
  BlogRepository.cs
  CodingBlogContext.cs
                                    Solution-wide analysis is off.
                                    Double-click for options.
  Ch 14          INS    233 MB
```

With enabled Solution-wide inspections, ReSharper can mark the public methods or returned values that are unused.

 Please note that running Solution-wide inspections can affect Visual Studio's performance during big projects. In such cases, it is better to disable this feature.

Disabling code inspections

With ReSharper v8, you can easily mark some part of your code as code that should not be checked by ReSharper.

You can do this by adding the following comments:

```
// ReSharper disable all
// [your code]
// ReSharper restore all
```

All code between these two comments will be skipped by ReSharper in code inspections. Of course, instead of the `all` word, you can use the name of any ReSharper rule such as `UseObjectOrCollectionInitializer`.

You can also disable ReSharper analysis for a single line with the following comment:

```
// ReSharper disable once UseObjectOrCollectionInitializer
```

ReSharper can generate these comments for you. If ReSharper highlights an issue, then just press *Alt + Enter* and select **Options for "YOUR_RULE" inspection**, as shown in the following screenshot:

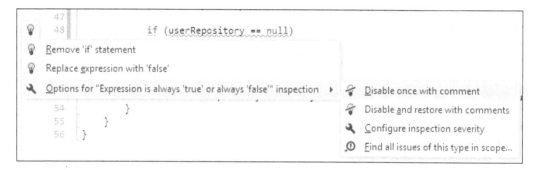

Code Issues

You can also an ad-hoc run code analysis. An ad-hoc analysis can be run on the solution or project level.

To run ad-hoc analysis, just navigate to **RESHARPER | Inspect | Code Issues in Solution** or **RESHARPER | Inspect | Code Issues in Current Project** from the Visual Studio toolbar.

This will display a dialog box that shows us the progress of analysis and will finally display the results in the **Inspection Results** window. You can filter and group the displayed issues as and when you need to. You can also quickly go to a place where the issue occurs just by double-clicking on it.

A sample report is shown in the following screenshot:

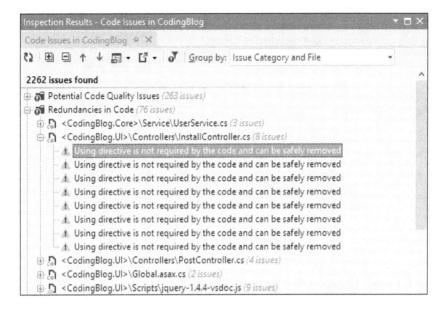

Eliminating errors and code smells

We think you will agree that the code analysis provided by ReSharper is really cool and helps create better code. What is even cooler is that ReSharper provides you with features that can fix some issues automatically.

Quick fixes

Most errors and issues found by ReSharper can be fixed just by pressing *Alt + Enter*. This will display a list of the available solutions and lets you select the best one for you.

Fix in scope

The quick fixes we just described allow you to fix the issues in one particular place. However, sometimes there are issues that you would like to fix in every file in your project or solution. A great example is removing unused `using` statements or the `this` keyword.

With ReSharper v8, you do not need to fix such issues manually. Instead, you can use a new feature called **Fix in scope**. You start as usual by pressing *Alt + Enter* but instead of just selecting a solution, you can select more options by clicking the small arrow on the right from the available options.

A sample usage of the Fix in scope feature is shown in the following screenshot:

This will allow you to fix the selected issue with just one click!

Structural Search and Replace

Even though ReSharper contains a lot of built-in analysis, it also allows you to create your own analyses. You can create your own patterns that will be used to search some structures in your code. This feature is called **Structural Search and Replace (SSR)**.

To open the **Search with Pattern** window, navigate to **RESHARPER | Find | Search with Pattern...**. A sample window is shown in the following screenshot:

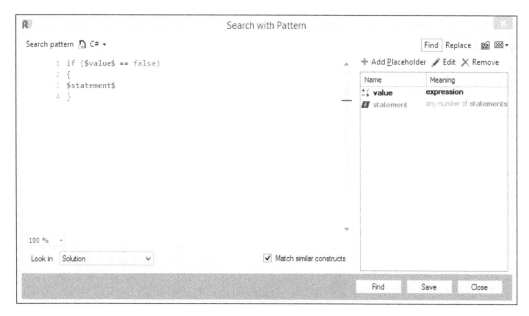

You can see two things here:

- On the left, there is a place to write your pattern
- On the right, there is a place to define **placeholders**

In the preceding example, we were looking for `if` statements to compare them with a `false` expression.

You can now simply click on the **Find** button and ReSharper will display every piece of code that matches this pattern. Of course, you can also save your patterns.

 You can create new search patterns from the code editor. Just select some code, click on the right mouse button, and select **Find Similar Code…**.This will automatically generate the pattern for this code, which you can easily adjust to your needs.

SSR allows you not only to find code based on defined patterns, but also replace it with different code. Click on the **Replace** button available on the top in the preceding screenshot. This will display a new section on the left called **Replace pattern**. There, you can write code that will be placed instead of code that matches the defined pattern.

For the pattern shown, you can write the following code:

```
if (false = $value$)
{
$statement$
}
```

This will simply change the order of expressions inside the `if` statement.

The saved patterns can also be presented as **Quick fixes**. Simply navigate to **RESHARPER | Options | Code Inspection | Custom Patterns** and set the right severity for your pattern, as shown in the following screenshot:

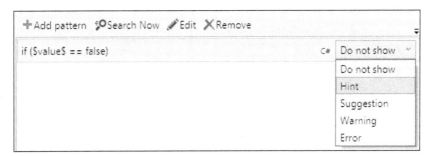

This will allow you to define patterns in the code editor, which is shown in the following screenshot:

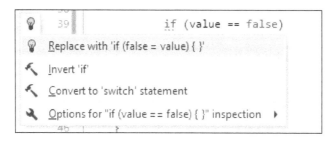

Code Cleanup

ReSharper also allows you to fix more than one issue in one run. Navigate to **RESHARPER | Tools | Cleanup Code...** in the Visual Studio toolbar or just press *Ctrl + E, Ctrl + C*. This will display the **Code Cleanup** window, which is shown in the following screenshot:

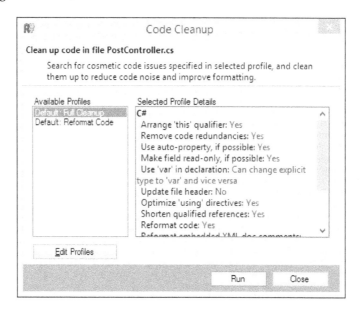

By clicking on the **Run** button, ReSharper will fix all issues configured in the selected profile. By default, there are two patterns:

- Full Cleanup
- Reformat Code

You can add your own pattern by clicking on the **Edit Profiles** button.

Summary

Code quality analysis is a very powerful feature in ReSharper. As we have described in this chapter, ReSharper not only prompts you when something is wrong or can be written better, but also allows you to quickly fix these issues.

If you do not agree with all rules provided by ReSharper, you can easily configure them to meet your needs.

There are many rules that will open your eyes and show you that you can write better code. With ReSharper, writing better, cleaner code is as easy as just pressing *Alt + Enter*.

In the next chapter, we will review features that support web development.

5
Extended Support for Web Developers

ReSharper has been focused on supporting backend languages such as C# or VB.NET from the beginning. Fortunately, with almost every release, there are more and more languages that are supported.

Currently, ReSharper provides you with many features that can be used by almost every .NET developer. Most of these features are dedicated to web developers.

In this chapter, we will explain how ReSharper supports the following:

- ASP.NET and ASP.NET MVC
- JavaScript
- TypeScript
- HTML/CSS

As we have described most of these features, here we will only quickly describe how they support web development without a detailed description.

 Some of the presented features already exist in newer versions of Visual Studio, but ReSharper adds these features to all supported versions.

ASP.NET Web Forms and ASP.NET MVC tools

In terms of web development in Visual Studio, ASP.NET was the first area that was supported by ReSharper. Currently, almost every ReSharper feature supports ASP.NET in some way—both Web Forms and MVC.

Writing ASP.NET smartly

In the same way as in C#, ReSharper helps you write ASP.NET by extending IntelliSense, generating code, and providing you with some refactoring methods.

IntelliSense provides you with prompts for web-related things, such as ASP.NET controls, ASP.NET MVC helpers, resources, JavaScript symbols, and so on.

While working with ASP.NET, ReSharper helps you in importing required namespaces and removing unused directives (same as with `using` statements in C#).

As with C#, ReSharper allows you to generate members based on the implemented interface; in ASP.NET, you can generate **Content** tags based on **ContentPlaceHolders** from your Master Page and the required event handlers.

Templates

When you are working with the ASP.NET project, ReSharper allows you to use file templates that are specific to ASP.NET. You can find templates to add web pages, controls, and Razor views, as shown in the following screenshot:

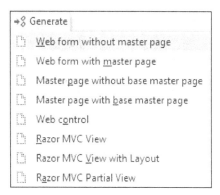

Quick reminder: creating a new file from a template can be done by pressing *Ctrl + Alt + Insert* from the code editor or by pressing *Alt + Insert* in **Solution Explorer**.

And of course, you can define your own templates.

Enhanced navigation

In case of navigation, you can find well-known features such as displaying the **File Structure** or navigation through file using the **Go to File Member** option by pressing *Alt + *. Using the **Go to File Member** option, you can search by HTML tags, IDs, CSS classes, and any other object used in your view. A sample search by HTML tag and element ID is shown in the following screenshot:

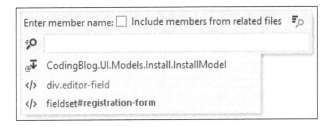

A very useful feature in web applications is **Go to Related Files**. You can access this option by pressing *Ctrl + Alt + F7*. It is also available in C# but is most useful in ASP.NET or HTML code. It allows you to quickly navigate to related files, such as JavaScript, CSS, Master Page, Controls, and any related code.

The following screenshot presents you with a list of related files for a sample ASP.NET MVC view:

As you can see, it contains the controller that is related to this view, the JavaScript files declared in this file, the master layout, and CSS files declared in this layout.

ASP.NET MVC specific support

In case of support for ASP.NET MVC, the most important feature is IntelliSense, which prompts you the controllers and controller's methods every time you need to specify them. A sample usage is shown in the following screenshot:

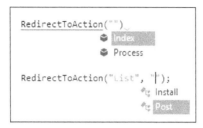

ReSharper also improves navigation between controllers and views, and detects non-existent views, as you can see in the following screenshot:

The preceding screenshot presents the `return` statement from the `Process` method.

 In Visual Studio, there's a very useful shortcut, *Ctrl* + *G, M*, which allows you to easily switch between View and Controller. Just put your cursor somewhere in the controller method or in the view method and use this shortcut.

Support for JavaScript

For a long time, writing JavaScript code in Visual Studio was very painful. There were no tools that could support writing JavaScript. But ReSharper changed this by providing you with a rich set of features that you know from C#.

 ReSharper supports JavaScript code, both written in separate files and inline in the same way.

Smart IntelliSense

Support for JavaScript starts with IntelliSense. IntelliSense prompts you with defined JavaScript keywords and methods, and objects and methods from your custom objects as well as from external JavaScript libraries such as jQuery. A sample prompt for jQuery methods is shown in the following screenshot:

```
<script>
    $('.myclass').
</script>              pushStack (in jquery-2.0.3.min.js)
                      queue (in jquery-2.0.3.min.js)
@using (Html.Be      ready (in jquery-2.0.3.min.js)
    @Html.Valic      reduce (in EcmaScript5.js)
    <fieldset>       reduceRight (in EcmaScript5.js)
        <legenc
```

> In jQuery, selectors are very important as they allow you to access any HTML element. ReSharper can help you with specifying selectors by providing you with a list of available CSS classes and HTML tags.

The Code Analysis and refactoring options

Another well-known ReSharper feature is Code Analysis. It allows you to quickly find and fix some common errors.

From this analysis, ReSharper will notify you when it will find any one of the following conditions:

- Unused or redundant code
- Duplicate labels in the `switch` statement or property declaration
- Statement not terminated with a semicolon
- Possibly unassigned property or variable

You can find a complete list of available **Code Inspections** in the ReSharper options by navigating to **Code Inspection | Inspection Severity** in the **JS** tab.

Together with Code Analysis, ReSharper comes with some simple refactoring methods for JavaScript. You will find options such as **Rename, Create from usage**, or **Introduce variable**.

All these features work in JavaScript in the same way as they work in C#.

Navigation and smart usages

With ReSharper, you can also easily review JavaScript code structure in the **File Structure** window. A sample structure is shown in the following screenshot:

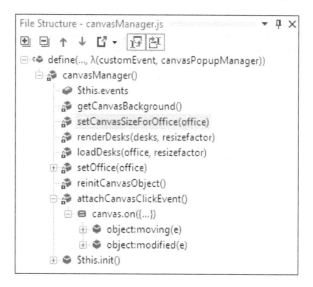

Same as in other languages, you can navigate between different type members in your file with the **Go to File Member** (*Alt + *) option and find code dependencies by finding the code declaration or code usage.

Structural Search and Replace (SSR)

Starting with ReSharper v8, you can use the SSR feature together with JavaScript code. You can find out more about this feature in *Chapter 4, Making Your Code Better*.

Support for TypeScript

As support for ASP.NET and JavaScript has been existing in ReSharper for some time, support for TypeScript is a new feature that comes with ReSharper v8.1.

TypeScript is a typed superset of JavaScript that compiles to plain JavaScript. It allows you to write JavaScript in manner that is similar to C#. As TypeScript is very similar to JavaScript, ReSharper comes with a very similar support for it.

Same as with JavaScript, ReSharper provides you with Smart IntelliSense and templates.

You can navigate through your code by navigating to the **File Structure | Go to File Member** options. You can find your code dependency and use some simple refactoring methods such as **Rename** or **Introduce Variable**.

Remember that ReSharper v8.1 is the first version to provide support for TypeScript, so you can be sure that future versions will come with more.

Support for HTML/CSS

ReSharper v6 was very web development friendly. Besides supporting JavaScript, it also started supporting HTML and CSS.

Writing HTML/CSS code

ReSharper comes with a couple of features that help you in writing HTML and CSS code.

The first feature is IntelliSense for HTML tags, attributes, CSS attributes, and values. In a very smart way, it prompts you about what you wish to probably write. These options are shown in the following screenshot:

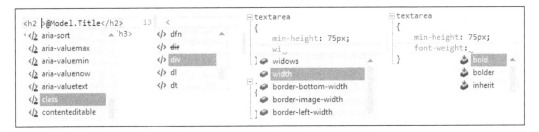

ReSharper can not only prompt defined CSS attributes, but also your custom CSS classes, as shown in the following screenshot:

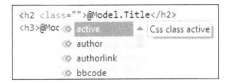

ReSharper analyzes your CSS files (and CSS inline code) and allows you to use created classes in your code. What is really cool is that ReSharper prompts these classes not only in HTML code, but also in ASP.NET (MVC) as well as JavaScript.

Additionally, ReSharper provides you with context actions that also help you in writing code. They allow you to remove HTML attributes, add tags, and quickly create the table structure. The following screenshot shows you how you can easily create new table rows:

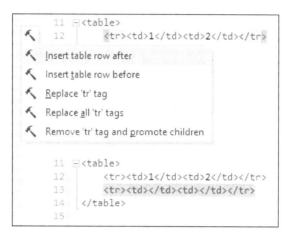

In the same way, you can create new columns.

If you would like to duplicate the whole line (in any type of file), just hover the cursor over that line and press *Ctrl + D*!

In the case of CSS, ReSharper comes with a set of context actions that allow you to convert different methods of presenting colors, such as named colors, hex, and RGB.

ReSharper also displays visually used colors any time you specify a color, as shown in the following screenshot:

```
.input-validation-error
{
    border: 1px solid #ff0000;
    background-color: yellow;
}
```

You can also adjust your color by using a palette color. Just move your cursor to the color definition, press *Alt + Enter*, and select **Pick color from palette**.

CSS hierarchy

CSS hierarchy is a very useful tool that shows you how CSS classes inherit from other classes. A sample view of the CSS hierarchy window is shown in the following screenshot:

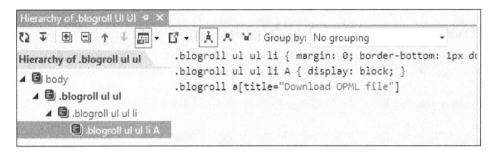

The CSS hierarchy makes it easier to understand which style will be applied to the HTML elements.

Navigation

Similar to other languages, you can display the file structure for HTML and CSS code as you can see in the following screenshot:

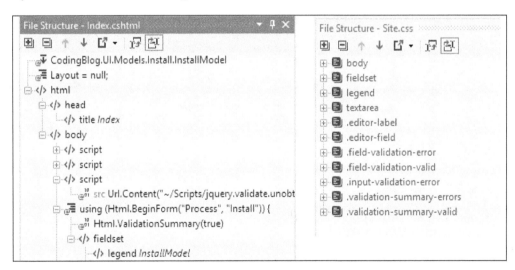

This helps you quickly go to the proper place in your file.

You can also search CSS classes with the **Go to everything** option (*Ctrl + T*) and use the **Go to declaration** or **Find usages** features to quickly check how your CSS class is declared and where it is used.

Go to file member (*Alt + *) works for both CSS and HTML code.

Browser compatibility support

There are a couple of CSS and HTML versions which may be supported by browsers a bit differently sometimes. ReSharper can check if your code is compatible with the CSS and HTML version that you are using as well as with specific versions of different browsers.

You can configure these settings in the ReSharper options by navigating to **Code Editing | CSS | Inspections**, as shown in the following screenshot:

Templates

You can also use templates in HTML and CSS code. From these templates, you can find the following tags:

- **t**: This generates open and close tags
- **tc**: This generates self-closing tags
- **<script**: This generates the script tag and automatically displays the list of available script types

You can check the list of available templates in the **Templates Explorer** window. You can find out more about templates in *Chapter 2, Write Smarter Code*.

Remember that you can create your own templates as you need!

 Surround With (*Ctrl + E, U*) is a very useful template that allows you to select some text and surround it with any HTML tag.

Code analysis

Code analysis is also available in HTML and CSS, where it can quickly find and fix some common errors, such as unknown tags and IDs, and unused, obsolete, or redundant code.

You can find the list of available code analysis in ReSharper options by navigating to **Code Inspection | Inspection Severity**.

Summary

As you can see, ReSharper comes with a very rich set of features that support web development. This makes creating web applications much friendlier.

The currently provided features allow you to work with JavaScript in almost the same way as with C# or VB.NET. The same goes for brand new TypeScript. We can use templates, a bunch of refactoring methods, and many more well-known features in ASP.NET. We can use these features even in simple languages such as HTML or CSS.

In the next chapter, we will focus on the ReSharper features that will help you in working with Unit Tests.

6
Unit Testing

ReSharper comes with a very user-friendly test runner which, by default, supports tests written with NUnit and MSTest as well as tests written for JavaScript.

As with any ReSharper feature, support for unit tests looks the same in all supported Visual Studio versions. Thanks to this, you can easily run NUnit and JavaScript unit tests in Visual Studio versions that only support MSTest.

In this chapter, we will cover the following topics:

- Test runner
- Testing JavaScript
- Analyzing code coverage with dotCover

Test runner

ReSharper provides you with the following two new windows that allow you to work with unit tests:

- **Unit Test Explorer**: To open this window, navigate to **RESHARPER | Windows | Unit Tests** from the Visual Studio menu or use the *Ctrl + Alt + U* shortcut

- **Unit Test Sessions**: To open this window, navigate to **RESHARPER | Windows | Unit Test Sessions** from the Visual Studio menu or use the *Ctrl + Alt + T* shortcut

Additionally, for new windows, the ReSharper test runner is integrated with the Code Editor in Visual Studio. It adds a new icon for every class that contains unit tests as well as for each particular test method, as shown in the following screenshot:

The first icon allows you to quickly run or debug all the tests in a class, and the second one allows you to run or debug particular tests.

Depending on the other tools that are installed, ReSharper also allows you to use other options such as profiling tests with dotTrace or checking code coverage with dotCover.

By default, ReSharper v8.1 comes with support for NUnit 2.6.3. This version of NUnit is built-in ReSharper and is used to run your tests. If you would like to use a different version of NUnit, you need to go to the NUnit configuration in ReSharper (**RESHARPER | Options | Tools | Unit Testing | NUnit**). These options are shown in the following screenshot:

ReSharper can also work with NUnit plugins—to use them, you need to put them into the folder shown in the previous screenshot.

ReSharper can also work with other unit test frameworks by installing proper plugins. A list of available plugins is present on the page at `https://resharper-plugins.jetbrains.com/packages?q=Tags:"unittest"`.

The Unit Test Explorer window

The **Unit Test Explorer** window displays all the unit tests found in your solution. ReSharper can automatically recognize the tests from supported frameworks.

This window also provides you with the same options as the menu that is integrated with the Code Editor, and allows you to run or debug tests and add tests to sessions.

A sample view of **Unit Test Explorer** is shown in the following screenshot:

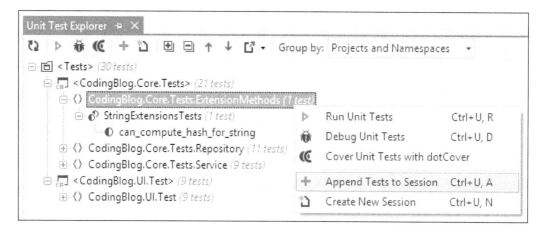

Apart from the menu options and icons shown in the preceding screenshot, you can run tests via shortcuts. Use *Ctrl + U, R* to run tests or *Ctrl + U, D* to debug them.

The Unit Test Sessions window

ReSharper runs all unit test in sessions. You can think about sessions as groups. When you click on the **Run Test** option, ReSharper automatically creates a new session for you. You can add as many sessions as you need and configure the tests that these sessions contain. This allows you to group unit tests according to your needs. For example, in one session, you can have a test for your routing table in ASP. NET MVC and in another session, you can have tests related to your business logic. Thanks to this, you can easily run the needed tests together even if they are placed in different files or projects.

You can quickly run unit tests from the current session by using the *Ctrl + U, Y* shortcut or all unit tests in the solution by using the *Ctrl + U, L* shortcut.

The **Unit Test Sessions** window is also the place where ReSharper displays test results. To make it easier to analyze failed tests, ReSharper displays the code of the failed tests and allows you to quickly navigate to the place at which the test failed, as shown in the following screenshot:

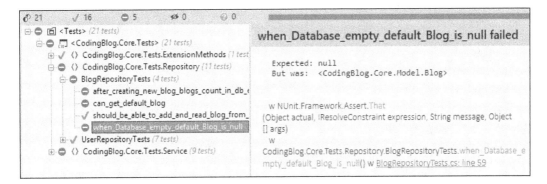

As with many other windows, in ReSharper, you can group and filter the displayed tests based on your needs. ReSharper also allows you to select the platform and .NET Framework version on which you would like to run the tests, as shown in the following screenshot:

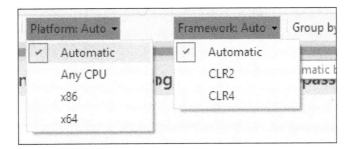

Testing JavaScript

ReSharper can also support you in writing unit tests in JavaScript.

Running JavaScript unit tests

There are many different frameworks that allow you to write unit tests for JavaScript. The most popular ones are **QUnit** and **Jasmine**. What is really cool is that both are supported by ReSharper. It means that you can run them in the same way that you run C# tests written in NUnit or other frameworks. Very nice, isn't it?

A sample unit test written in QUnit is shown in the following screenshot:

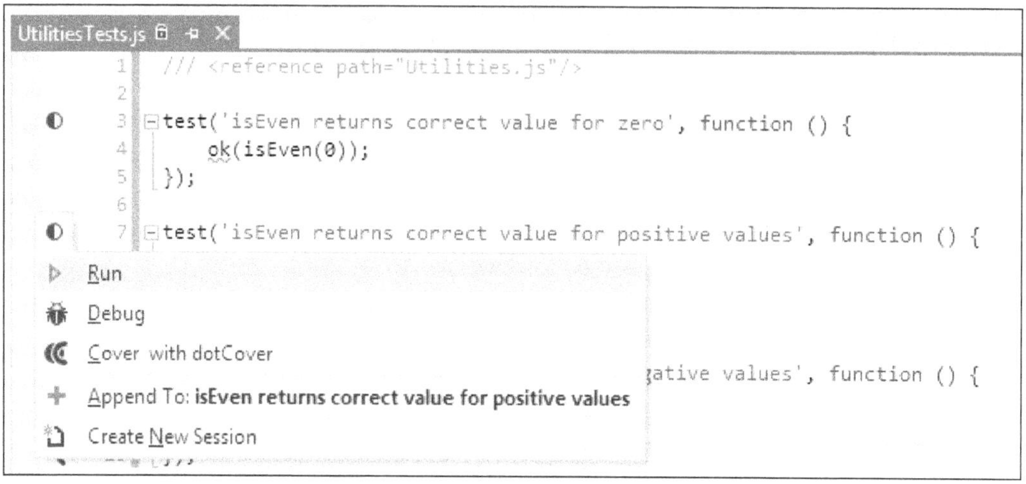

As you can see, ReSharper recognizes and marks unit tests in the same way as they were with NUnit. Even the available menu options are the same.

When you write unit tests in JavaScript, you need to add a reference to the file that contains the tested methods. You can see a sample reference in the previous screenshot, which looks as follows:

```
/// <reference path="Utilities.js"/>
```

ReSharper needs to know where the code that you are testing is placed. You do the same in C# but with the `using` statement.

As we talk about testing JavaScript code that is created for web applications, ReSharper is running these tests in a web browser. That is why ReSharper will automatically open your default browser to run the tests. Normally, when you are writing unit tests in QUnit, you need to add an HTML file that contains a QUnit runner and displays results. With ReSharper, you do not need to do this as ReSharper handles this internally.

A sample report displayed in a web browser after running the unit test looks similar to the following screenshot:

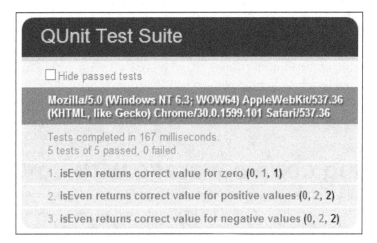

You can select the browser in which you would like to run tests in ReSharper. These settings are shown in the following screenshot:

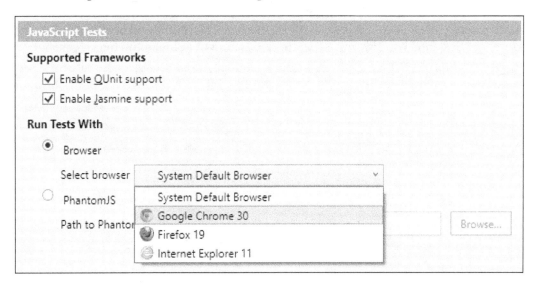

Integration with PhantomJS

ReSharper allows you to run JavaScript tests outside the browser. This is made possible by adding support for **PhantomJS**. PhantomJS is a type of web browser but without the user interface (also known as headless browser) and is based on the WebKit engine. It may sound weird but it makes PhantomJS a very powerful tool. It is available as a command-line tool, so it is easy to integrate PhantomJS with different tools such as ReSharper. To use PhantomJS with ReSharper, you need to download it from `http://phantomjs.org`, unpack it, and set the path to the `phantomjs.exe` file in the settings window shown previously.

Analyzing code coverage with dotCover

As we mentioned previously in this chapter, ReSharper can work together with dotCover — another great tool created by JetBrains. dotCover is a code coverage tool that can work independently of ReSharper but it can be also used together with it.

dotCover simply analyzes your code and presents a report that shows how much of your code is covered by unit tests.

To run dotCover from ReSharper, select **Cover Unit Tests with dotCover** from any place where you can run unit tests with ReSharper. The report will be displayed in the **Unit Test Sessions** window in a separate tab, as shown in the following screenshot:

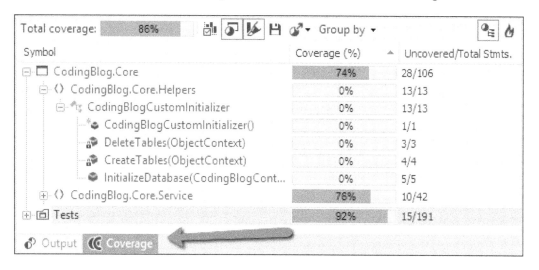

 You can read more about dotCover on the JetBrains website at `http://www.jetbrains.com/dotcover/`.

Summary

In this chapter, we have presented how ReSharper supports working with unit tests in Visual Studio.

ReSharper not only comes with a new, more user-friendly and configurable test runner, but also provides you with support for frameworks other than MSTest, regardless of the Visual Studio version used. ReSharper allows you to run unit tests written in JavaScript and, thanks to its integration with PhantomJS, allows you to run these tests without opening the web browser.

You have also learned how to check code coverage with dotCover—a separate tool provided by JetBrains.

In the next chapter, you will learn how to write a sample plugin for ReSharper.

7
Extending ReSharper

ReSharper comes with a robust set of features; users are able to add new features to it according to their needs. This chapter serves as a basic introduction to extending ReSharper and is a step-by-step guide for creating a sample plugin.

In this chapter, we will explain:

- Why you should extend ReSharper
- How the ReSharper API looks
- What the Internal mode is and how to enable the ReSharper Internal mode
- How to create your own plugin

Additionally, we will quickly go through a sample project provided with the ReSharper SDK.

ReSharper provides a couple of ways to extend its functionality; in this chapter, we will focus on writing plugins.

Why you should extend ReSharper

When we talk about extending ReSharper, you might wonder why you should do this. As ReSharper extends Visual Studio, why should you extend ReSharper and not Visual Studio?

To answer this, let's check how we can extend ReSharper. The following are the four ways to do it:

- Live templates
- Structural Search and Replace
- External annotations
- Plugins

We have already described the first two methods in the previous chapters. They just provide new rules to the existing ReSharper features, so this gives us a clear picture about why they are related to extending ReSharper. The same is the case with external annotations; they provide new rules for the code analysis feature.

 External annotations are not in the scope of this book. You can read more about this topic on the **ReSharper Web Help** page at `http://www.jetbrains.com/resharper/webhelp/Code_Analysis__External_Annotations.html`.

The last option, that is, plugins, are the most powerful as they are not strongly associated with just one feature. They do not even need to be related to ReSharper.

So, the question arises, why should you write plugins for ReSharper? The answer is, because it is easy. ReSharper comes with a very extensive API, which provides many useful features. Of course, we do not think that writing plugins for Visual Studio does not make sense. However, sometimes it is much easier to use features that already exist in ReSharper than write a custom one from scratch.

In your plugin, you can do everything that ReSharper does as you have access to the same API. With your plugin, you can not only create some new features but also add support for new languages or a new unit test framework.

The only disadvantage when we are thinking about plugins for ReSharper is that it limits the number of potential users, and our users need to have ReSharper.

The ReSharper API

ReSharper provides **Open API**, which is the same API that has been used to create all the features of ReSharper.

 As we would like to introduce you to only some basic concepts related to creating plugins in this book, we will quickly describe only the most important ones.

From an architectural point of view, the ReSharper API is divided into the following three layers:

- Platform
- **Program Structure Interface (PSI)**
- Features

When you are working on a plugin project, you can easily find the related assemblies based on their names, which are as follows:

- `JetBrains.Platform.ReSharper.*`
- `JetBrains.ReSharper.Psi.*`
- `JetBrains.ReSharper.Features.*` and `JetBrains.ReSharper.Feature.Services.*`

The hierarchy of these levels is presented in the following screenshot:

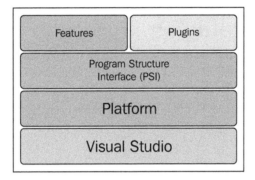

It is important to understand the responsibilities of these layers.

Platform

Platform is the first base layer, which allows you to work directly with the Visual Studio API.

The most important modules that you can find here are as follows:

- **Project model**: This is used to work with the Visual Studio project
- **Text control**: This allows you to work with the Visual Studio editor
- **Utils**: This provides some useful tools for reading/writing XML, specialized collections, filesystem path, and so on
- **Component model**: This provides the ReSharper IoC container

In the case of the component model, there are two types of components: shell components (created when the Visual Studio shell is created) and solution components (created when the Visual Studio solution is opened).

Program Structure Interface (PSI)

PSI is the most used layer as it serves as a parser for languages supported by ReSharper. It builds **Abstract Syntax Tree (AST)**, which you can access and navigate to through your plugin.

Features and plugins

In the top level, we have the features and plugins that we can see in ReSharper, such as navigation, code competition, and live templates. As you can see, built-in features are on the same level as plugins, which means that you, as a plugin developer, have access to the same methods as JetBrains developers, who create new features.

Daemons

Additionally, you can find `JetBrains.ReSharper.Daemon.*` assemblies, which are responsible for background tasks and code analysis.

Internal mode

We can run ReSharper in a special mode called the **Internal mode** (sometimes called god mode). This mode provides you with access to some tools and commands that are very useful when you are creating plugins.

In the Internal mode, two new options are available.

The first provides new entries in the **Options** window. These entries are as follows:

- **Tools | SolBuilderDuo**: This allows you to change the settings related to building plugins
- **Internal**: This allows you to change the settings related to exceptions, logging, and the tracking activity
- **Internal UI Options**: This allows to you change UI-related settings

The second one is a new option, **Internal**, in the ReSharper menu as presented in the following screenshot:

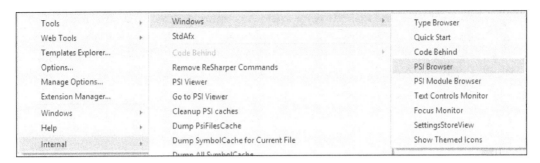

In this menu, you can find a lot of useful options. The most useful are as follows:

- **PSI Browser**: This can be found by navigating to **Internal | Windows**
- **PSI Module Browser**: This can be found by navigating to **Internal | Windows**
- **PSI Viewer**: This is available directly in the **Internal** menu

PSI Browser

PSI Browser is one of the most useful options. It allows you to review the PSI tree for the currently opened file.

A sample **PSI Browser** window is shown in the following screenshot:

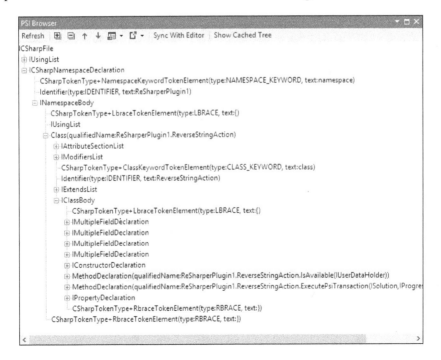

As you can easily see, the **PSI Browser** window contains a tree structure for the C# file. There are two separate nodes for using statements and the namespace. As tree nodes expand, you can see more code details with all the information needed for creating plugins.

Reviewing **PSI Browser** is the best way to learn about PSI tree structure and PSI types.

PSI Module Browser

The **PSI Module Browser** window allows you to review all the modules (assemblies) in your project and track the references between them, as shown in the following screenshot:

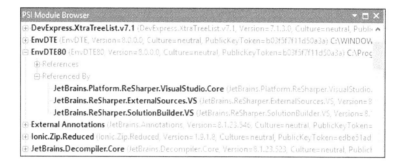

As you can see in the preceding screenshot, each module contains two nodes, **References** and **Referenced By**, which show the relations with other modules (for example, EnvDTE80 library is referenced by the `JetBrains.ReSharper.SolutionBuilder.vs` library).

PSI Viewer

The **PSI Viewer** window is very similar to **PSI Browser** with a single change; it allows you to write code snippets and check how code is represented as a PSI tree.

Remember that you have full access to all the information available on the **PSI Viewer** window via the ReSharper SDK, and you can use it in your plugin.

Enabling the Internal mode

To run ReSharper in the Internal mode, you need to run Visual Studio with the `/ReSharper.Internal` parameter. You can add this parameter to the **Target** field in the Visual Studio shortcut properties as presented in the following screenshot:

Or, you can just write the following line in the command line:

```
devenv.exe /ReSharper.Internal
```

The ReSharper SDK

To write plugins for ReSharper, you need to have the **Software Development Kit (SDK)** installed. Starting from ReSharper v8.1, SDK is divided into two parts, which we'll be discussing in the following sections.

Installing the ReSharper SDK

The first part of the SDK is the MSI installer, which contains Visual Studio project templates, item templates, and samples.

Installing the ReSharper SDK is very easy and can be done by performing the following steps:

1. Download the installation package. Go to the **Download ReSharper** page at `http://www.jetbrains.com/resharper/download/index.html` and click on **ReSharper SDK for ReSharper 8.1.x (.msi)** in the **Related Downloads** section.

2. After opening the downloaded installation package, you should see the standard installation screen. By clicking on the **Next** button, you can start the installation process.

3. After performing the previous step, you can open the `ReadMe.html` file, which contains a quick introduction to creating ReSharper plugins.

Getting the required NuGet packages

The second part of SDK contains all the assemblies that need to be referenced in the plugin project, MSBuild tasks, and all the required build tools. It is available as a NuGet package, as shown in the following screenshot:

As you can see, there are actually two packages. The first one contains the assemblies required to create plugins, and the second one contains assemblies to create tests for plugins.

Your first plugin

Now let's create your first plugin! In this example, we will use a plugin that is created automatically when you are creating a ReSharper plugin project. It simply allows you to reverse strings by adding a new context action and shows how you can add custom options to different menus in Visual Studio.

Creating a project

Assuming that you have installed SDK, we need to start with opening Visual Studio. It is important to run Visual Studio as an administrator.

Now let's create a new project. From the Visual Studio menu, navigate to **FILE | New Project** and from the **New Project** window, navigate to **Installed | Templates | Visual C# | ReSharper | v8.1**. This will display a list of the types of projects available to create the ReSharper plugin. Let's select **ReSharper Plugin**.

It is very important for you to select the correct version of the .NET Framework. If you select Version 4.0 or higher, your plugin will be able to work only with Visual Studio 2010 or higher. If you would like to support older versions of Visual Studio, you need to select the .NET Framework 3.5.

Enter a name for your plugin, that is, `AwesomeReSharperExtension`, set a location, and click on **OK**.

Visual Studio will ask you to provide some information about your plugin such as the title, description, and author. Provide some descriptions in the correct fields and click on **OK**.

Now let's rebuild your solution to confirm that everything is working as it should. When building a plugin for the first time, ReSharper will ask you which build engine you would like to use, as shown in the following screenshot:

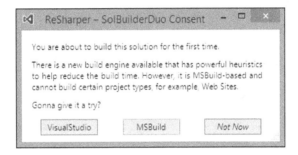

Click on **VisualStudio**. You can change this setting later on in the ReSharper **Options** window by navigating to the **Tools | SolBuilderDuo** screen.

As a project template comes with a reference to the ReSharper NuGet package, you do not need to add any references.

Project elements

Your project now contains the following four important files:

- `AssemblyInfo.cs` in the `Properties` folder
- `AboutAction.cs`
- `Actions.xml`
- `ReverseStringAction.cs`

Assembly info

Let's start with the first file, that is, `AssemblyInfo.cs`. It contains some metadata about your project. The plugin's related data contains information that you provided while creating a project and a file that contains a setting to add new actions to different menus:

```
[assembly: ActionsXml("AwesomeReSharperExtension.Actions.xml")]
```

In this case, these actions are stored in the `Actions.xml` file in our project (`AwesomeReSharperExtension`).

Actions

Now let's open the `Actions.xml` file. This XML file contains the definition to add new options for different menus.

It starts with the `<action>` node, which can contain sets of the `<action>` (for defining a new action) and `<insert>` (for inserting a new option in the menu, or creating a new action, or using the one created with the `<action>` attribute) elements.

Our sample file looks like what is shown in the following screenshot:

```xml
1    <?xml version="1.0" encoding="utf-8" ?>
2  ⊟<actions>
3  ⊟  <insert group-id="ReSharper" position="last">
4  ⊟    <action-group id="AwesomeReSharperExtension" text="AwesomeReSharperExtension">
5        <action id="AwesomeReSharperExtension.About" text="About Awesome ReSharper Extension"/>
6        <!-- to break up elements use <separator/> -->
7      </action-group>
8    </insert>
9  </actions>
```

In the third line, we are referencing the ReSharper menu option, which is displayed in the Visual Studio menu. We are also setting the position of the new entry that we would like to add in the menu option—this will be the last position. Inside the `<insert>` attribute, we are creating a new menu option, `AwesomeReSharperExtension`, with the submenu `About Awesome ReSharper Extension`. We are also setting a handler for the action `AwesomeReSharperExtension.About`.

When you want to add new menu options, you can reference different options as follows:

- **ReSharper.Navigate**: This will add a new option to the **Navigate** menu in the **RESHARPER** tab
- **VS#Solution**: This will add a new option to the menu, which is available after right-clicking on your solution name
- **VS#Project**: This will add a new option to the menu, which is available after right-clicking on your project name

As we know that our action will be handled by the `AwesomeReSharperExtension.About` handler, let's open the `AboutAction.cs` file.

Do you remember the *Ctrl + T* shortcut? Let's use it!

The `AboutAction` class looks like what is shown in the following screenshot:

```
[ActionHandler("AwesomeReSharperExtension.About")]
public class AboutAction : IActionHandler
{
    public bool Update(IDataContext context, ActionPresentation presentation, DelegateUpdate nextUpdate)[...]

    public void Execute(IDataContext context, DelegateExecute nextExecute)[...]
}
```

As you can see, this class starts with `ActionHandler`, which contains a name that we used in the `Actions.xml` file. Each action class needs to implement the `IActionHandler` interface. This interface comes with the following two methods:

- `Update()`: This method returns a boolean value, which tells ReSharper if our action is disabled/enabled
- `Execute()`: This method runs when our action is executed

In our case, the `Execute()` method just displays a simple message box.

Finally, our action looks like what is shown in the following screenshot:

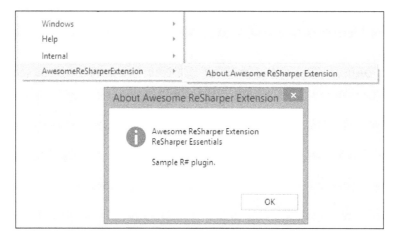

Context action

The most interesting feature of our plugin is the context action that can reverse strings.

Let's check the `ReverseStringAction` class. As you can see, it inherits from the `ContextActionBase` class and has the `ContextAction` attribute as shown in the following screenshot:

```
[ContextAction(Name = "ReverseString", Description = "Reverses a string", Group = "C#")]
public class ReverseStringAction : ContextActionBase
{
```

Values from the `ContextAction` attribute are used for displaying this context action in the ReSharper **Options** window.

Our class overrides the following two methods and one property:

- `IsAvailable()`
- `ExecutePsiTransaction()`
- `Text`

The `Text` property returns the name that will be displayed on the list of available context actions.

The `IsAvailable()` method informs ReSharper if our action is available in a specific context. This method is run every time you move your cursor in the text editor.

In this method, the two most important lines are shown in the following screenshot:

```
var literal = _provider.GetSelectedElement<ILiteralExpression>(true, true);
if (literal != null && literal.IsConstantValue() && literal.ConstantValue.IsString())
{
```

The first line gets the element that is currently under the cursor. We are interested only in literal expressions (which are strings, numbers, and so on), so we are limiting the searched elements by the `ILiteralExpression` interface.

 You can check the type of any object in your code in the **PSI Browser** window.

The second line checks if the element is a string value. This means that our context action will be available only if we place the cursor on a string (but not on the variable, which is a `string` type).

The second method, `ExecutePsiTransaction()`, is run when the user selects our action. It simply reverses the string (which we found in the `IsAvailable()` method) and replaces it in the code editor.

Other project elements

You can add more objects to your plugin. ReSharper SDK adds some item templates; for example, Context Action, Live Template Macro, and Quick Fix, which you can access by clicking on the right mouse button on your project, navigating to **Add | New Item...**, and filtering the available items to ReSharper items.

Each item contains some sample code that you can use in your plugin.

Debugging a plugin

If you started developing a plugin using the ReSharper template, debugging it is quite easy — just press *F5*.

This is possible as the template contains proper debugging configuration, which you can see in the following screenshot:

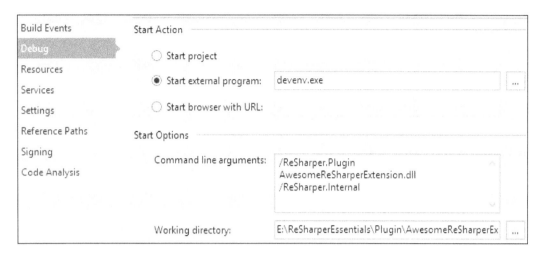

You can navigate to this screen from your project settings. The important part is setting devenv.exe (Visual Studio) as the start program and setting two command line arguments: /ReSharper.Plugin, which loads your plugin, and /ReSharper. Internal, which we have described earlier in this chapter. Finally, it is important to set **Working directory**, so we will need to specify only the filename and not the complete path to our plugin's .dll file.

Deploying a plugin

Starting from ReSharper 8, plugins are provided as NuGet packages. To deploy a new plugin, you need to create a new NuGet package and upload it onto the ReSharper gallery at http://resharper-plugins.jetbrains.com.

Creating NuGet packages is not in the scope of this book. For more information, you can check the NuGet documentation site at http://docs.nuget.org, or the **ReSharper Plugin Development** page at http://confluence.jetbrains.com/ display/NETCOM/ReSharper+Plugin+Development.

Your plugin in action

You already know how to debug and deploy your plugin. Additionally, if you would like to run it locally, you can just copy your `.dll` file to the `Bin/Plugins` folder in the main `ReSharper` folder.

If you run Visual Studio with your plugin, you can access context action, as shown in the following screenshot:

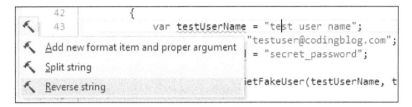

Sample SDK plugins

Along with Visual Studio templates, the ReSharper SDK installs sample plugins. They are available at `C:\Program Files (x86)\JetBrains\ReSharper\v8.1\` `SDK` (if you have 64-bit Windows) and `C:\Program Files\JetBrains\ReSharper\` `v8.1\SDK` (if you have 32-bit Windows).

In SDK you can find the following three plugins:

- **Sample plugin**: This presents some basic concepts related to creating custom actions, context actions, background analysis, and extending options.

- **ReSharper PowerToys**: This is divided into a couple of projects and presents more advanced features. Notice that there is no one solution that contains all these projects.

- **Psi plugin**: This presents basic concepts related with developing support for new languages in ReSharper.

You can find more information about these projects in the `ReadMe.html` file, which is placed together with samples.

Summary

ReSharper comes with many ways of extending its functionality, from simply adding new templates to creating advanced plugins.

JetBrains provides many tools that make it easier to create plugins for ReSharper—SDK, samples, and the Internal mode are very powerful and useful tools.

Creating plugins for a big tool such as ReSharper is a very vast topic and can be described in detail in a separate book. This means that it is not possible to give you all the information in one chapter. The purpose of this chapter was to show you the basic concepts related to creating the ReSharper plugin and start thinking about your amazing plugins.

If you would like to learn more about how to write ReSharper plugins, you can visit the **ReSharper Plugin Development** page at `http://confluence.jetbrains.com/display/NETCOM/ReSharper+Plugin+Development` and review the plugins provided with SDK samples. Also, there are a couple of open source plugins that you can find at `http://github.com` or `http://www.codeplex.com`.

In the next chapter, we will learn how ReSharper can help architects.

8
Tools for Architects

From the beginning, ReSharper was created to support developers in their work. ReSharper v8 comes with a new tool for viewing project dependencies, which can be very helpful for architects.

In this chapter, we will cover the following topics:

- Architecture View
- Advanced references view
- Global refactoring

Architecture View

While developers are focused mostly on the detailed implementation of projects, architects need a bird's-eye view of it.

ReSharper v8 comes with a new tool, **Architecture View**. Architecture View is a graph that presents the dependencies between projects in your solution. You can find a similar tool in Visual Studio Ultimate, but with ReSharper, you do not need to have this most expensive version.

Projects on this graph can be grouped based on solution folders. You can hide unimportant projects and display only dependent or referenced projects. Architecture View allows you to configure the displayed graph to provide the needed perspective.

Architecture View also presents the strength of the relation between two projects. You can easily see this by looking at the thickness of the lines linking the projects — a thicker line means a stronger relation, which means that there are more objects used between these two projects.

Architecture View can be useful for small solutions (with just a couple of projects), but the more projects you have, the more useful it will be for you.

The simple Architecture View is shown in the following screenshot:

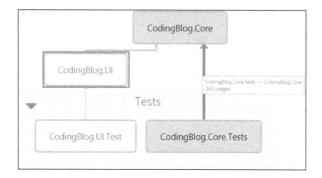

The slightly darker area, labeled **Tests**, is a group that contains two projects that are in the solution folder **Tests**. If you have a good folder structure in your solution, you can analyze references between different layers/modules as you collapse these groups and only check contained projects if needed.

You can also save your graphs any time and compare them later, so you can quickly check what has changed in your solution.

Advanced references view

The graph presented in Architecture View allows you to check the dependencies overview in your solution; it also provides additional tools which come with more detailed information.

The Referenced Code window

One of these tools is called **Referenced Code**. Click the right mouse button on your project (from **Architecture View**) and select **Navigate To...** | **Referenced Code**.

This will open the **Referenced Code** window as shown in the following screenshot:

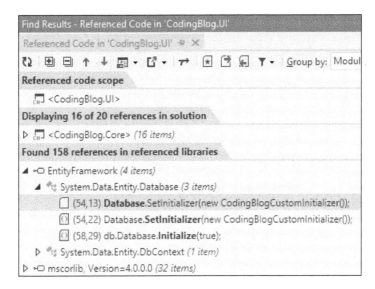

This window presents a list of all the assemblies used by a selected project. Projects from your solution and external libraries are displayed separately.

 If there are some assemblies that are referenced by your project but are not used, they will not be displayed in the **Referenced Code** window.

The **Referenced Code** window allows you to check the number of places you are using code from a particular assembly and the line this code has used.

The Optimize References window

The next tool is the **Optimize References** window. You can access it by clicking the right mouse button on your project (from **Architecture View**) and selecting **Optimize References...**.

Unlike **Referenced Code**, **Optimize References** displays all referenced assemblies. It also allows you to check the number of places you are using code from a particular assembly, and additionally marks assemblies that are referenced but not used.

Global refactoring

Architecture tools not only allow you to analyze references between different modules, but also fix some global issues.

A list of available refactoring options can be accessed from the **Refactor This** menu option, as shown in the following screenshot:

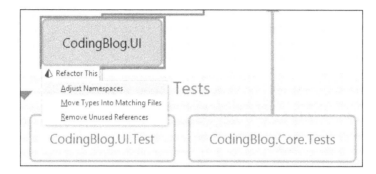

As you can see, you can easily adjust namespaces, move classes into separate files, and remove unused references in different modules.

Summary

Architecture tools provided by ReSharper present you with a global view of your project. You can easily check references between different modules and quickly fix some issues.

Such a high perspective view makes it easier to find rules in your architecture that have been broken, such as undesirable references, and provide code with better quality.

In the next chapter, we will see how you can use ReSharper without Visual Studio.

9
Code Analysis Beyond Visual Studio

ReSharper v8 comes with brand new, free command-line tools to run code analysis outside Visual Studio.

The tools come as a compressed package. To download them, go to the **Download ReSharper** page at http://www.jetbrains.com/resharper/download/ and click on **ReSharper Command Line Tools** in the **Related Downloads** section. When you unpack this package, you will find many .dll files in there that come from ReSharper and also the following two important .exe files:

- dupfinder.exe: This finds code duplicates
- inspectcode.exe: This runs code analysis

In this chapter, we will quickly describe these applications.

Finding code duplicates

The first tool, **dupfinder**, can be used to find duplicates in your C# and VB.NET code. What is really cool is that it not only marks some parts of your code as duplicated if they are identical, but also if they have a similar structure. This means that even if two parts of your code contain different variable names or methods, they can be, in a very smart way, marked as duplicated.

To run dupfinder, use the following command:

```
dupFinder [OPTIONS] source
```

The source parameter specifies what you would like to analyze. It can be a solution file or just files from your projects. A sample file path would look as follows:

```
dupfinder.exe E:\ctv_project\codingblog\trunk\src\CodingBlog.sln

dupfinder.exe E:\ctv_project\codingblog\trunk\src\**\*.cs
```

At the end, dupfinder will inform you of how many files have been analyzed and where the report has been created through the following output:

```
26 files found to analyze.

INFO: Duplicates report was written to
   C:\Users\Lukasz\AppData\Local\Temp\tmp9D32.tmp
```

By default, it is saved in the Temp folder, but you can change this with the /output option.

For more options that you can use with dupfinder, run the following command:

```
dupfinder /help
```

With additional options, you can exclude some files, check CPU usage and memory statistics, use debug messages, include duplicated code, and more.

A sample report is shown in the following screenshot:

```xml
<?xml version="1.0" encoding="utf-8"?>
<DuplicatesReport ToolsVersion="8.1">
  <Statistics>
    <CodebaseCost>7180</CodebaseCost>
    <TotalDuplicatesCost>242</TotalDuplicatesCost>
    <TotalFragmentsCost>484</TotalFragmentsCost>
  </Statistics>
  <Duplicates>
    <Duplicate Cost="85">
      <Fragment>
        <FileName>..\ctv_project\src\CodingBlog.Service.Tests\Repository\UserRepositoryTests.cs</FileName>
        <OffsetRange Start="2130" End="2456" />
        <LineRange Start="60" End="67" />
      </Fragment>
      <Fragment>
        <FileName>..\ctv_project\src\CodingBlog.Service.Tests\Repository\UserRepositoryTests.cs</FileName>
        <OffsetRange Start="3142" End="3468" />
        <LineRange Start="82" End="89" />
      </Fragment>
    </Duplicate>
  </Duplicates>
```

As it is available as an XML file, you can use an XSL transformation to convert it into an HTML report or use any custom tool to prepare the required report.

Running code analysis

The second tool, **Inspectcode** can be used to run the ReSharper code analysis.

To use Inspectcode, just run the following command:

```
InspectCode [options] [project file]
```

As with the `[project file]` parameter, specify the path to your solution file.

You can check the list of all the available options with the following command:

```
Inspectcode /help
```

Like with dupfinder, Inspectcode saves a report to the **Temp** folder by default, and you can change this location with the `/output` option.

The report is generated as an XML file and contains the following two parts:

- A list of all types of issues found during analysis with their severity and the link to the Wikipedia page (if available) that contains more information on the issue
- A list of all the issues grouped by projects with a specified file and the line in which the issue occurs

Inspectcode will use code analysis settings from a `.DotSettings` file, if it finds one in your project. With additional options, you can specify which project from your solution you would like to analyze, and choose if you would like to use solution-wide analysis and more.

TeamCity

For some time now, both these tools are available in the TeamCity, Continuous Integration tool developed by JetBrains.

 You can use these tools on every new commit that is sent to the repository managed by TeamCity.

You can get more information about this tool, and even get the free version, at `http://www.jetbrains.com/teamcity/`.

Summary

ReSharper is helpful not only in developing applications with Visual Studio, but you can also run it outside, where you can use code inspections and find duplicates in your code. This allows you to integrate these two ReSharper features with almost every application. It will be most useful for you to use it with your Continuous Integration tool, but you can also easily convert results to HTML or prepare any custom report tool. This makes these free tools very powerful.

In the next chapter, we will check some useful plugins that extend the standard ReSharper features.

10
Recommended Plugins

ReSharper comes with many useful features. However, there is always room for more. As we described in *Chapter 7, Extending ReSharper*, ReSharper can be extended quite easily using plugins, and there are many interesting plugins that you can use.

We will cover the following topics in this chapter:

- The ReSharper gallery
- Recommended plugins

The ReSharper gallery

Starting with ReSharper v8, plugins can be installed via the NuGet package manager. You can access it by navigating to **RESHARPER | Extension Manager ...** from the Visual Studio menu. A sample view of this window is shown in the following screenshot:

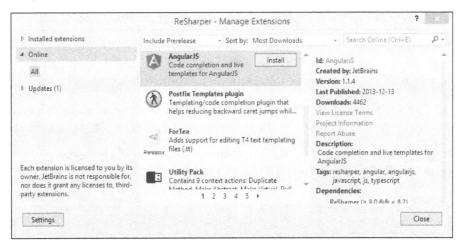

The **Extension Manager** window allows you to find, install, and update any plugin available in the ReSharper gallery. You can also review these plugins via the web page at http://resharper-plugins.jetbrains.com/.

If you are using a ReSharper version older than v8, you can still use the plugins; however, you will need to install them using the installation package provided by the developer of the plugin.

xUnit.net tests support

As we described in *Chapter 6, Unit Testing*, ReSharper contains a very good unit test runner. By default, it supports NUnit and MSTest.

If you are a fan of the xUnit library, you can also use the ReSharper test runner by installing the xUnit.net Contrib plugin.

It allows ReSharper to discover xUnit.net tests and adds a couple of **external annotations**, which extend the code analysis made by ReSharper.

It also provides very useful live templates, which speed up the writing of the tests.

More information about this plugin can be found at http://resharper-plugins. jetbrains.com/packages/xunitcontrib/ and http://xunitcontrib.codeplex. com, where you will find the available live templates.

Mnemonic Live Templates

The next plugin we would like to recommend is the Mnemonic Live Templates for C# and VB.NET.

It provides a set of incredibly useful live templates that generate code using structured abbreviations.

You can use c for creating classes, i for interfaces, m for methods, v for fields, and p for properties. By using a capital letter, you can create static objects.

You can also specify a return type with a second letter. For example, pi will create a property that returns int, ps will return string, pby will return byte, and so on.

By using the ~ sign, you can specify collections as return types. For example, p~s will create a property that returns a collection of strings.

Really awesome, isn't it?

Using these templates is very intuitive, and you can review a list of newly added templates in the **Templates Explorer** window by filtering the mnemonics category.

More information about this plugin can be found at
`https://resharper-plugins.jetbrains.com/packages/mnemonics/`.

Support for AngularJS

AngularJS is a very popular MVC JavaScript framework used to create **Single Page Applications**.

The AngularJS plugin adds support for this framework by providing code competition for AngularJS HTML attributes and live templates, which helps you in writing JavaScript code. For example, you can use the `ngc` template to generate an Angular controller, or `ngfor` to generate angular for each loop.

More information about the AngularJS plugin can be found at
`https://resharper-plugins.jetbrains.com/packages/AngularJS/`.

JSLint for ReSharper

JSLint for ReSharper is another plugin that supports development in JavaScript. It just adds support for the JSLint tool.

JSLint is a static code analyzer that looks for common bugs and bad practices in JavaScript. With the JSLint for ReSharper plugin installed, all the rules are highlighted in the same way as all ReSharper code analysis rules.

More details on JSLint for ReSharper can be found on the **ReSharper gallery** page at `https://resharper-plugins.jetbrains.com/packages/Resharper.JSLint/`.

The Utility Pack

The last plugin that we would like to recommend is the Utility Pack.

The current version, 1.0.2, adds nine new context actions, which are as follows:

- Duplicate Method
- Make Abstract
- Make Virtual
- Pull Parameters
- Reverse For-loop

- Use As Operation
- Use Cast Operation
- Use String.Compare
- Use StringBuilder

Again, a simple and very useful tool.

You can find out more about it at
`http://resharper-plugins.jetbrains.com/packages/UtilityPack/`.

Summary

As you can see, you can add many interesting features with ReSharper plugins. You can add more useful live templates and support for a new unit test framework and even new libraries. If you notice, we have described only five plugins.

There are more plugins that can be useful for you. You can review the ReSharper plugins gallery and check which plugins will be useful in your work. And remember, when you cannot find a plugin that you need, you can always create it yourself!

Keyboard Shortcuts

Almost every ReSharper action can be executed via a keyboard shortcut. Learning and practically using these shortcuts can incredibly speed up your coding.

 It is a good practice to learn keyboard shortcuts for the tools that you use often. It helps you avoid moving your hands between the keyboard and mouse and speeds up your work. So, every day learn at least one new shortcut and become a **Keyboard Ninja**!

This appendix provides a list of the most useful shortcuts presented in this book. You can find more ReSharper shortcuts on the **ReSharper Documentation** page at http://www.jetbrains.com/resharper/documentation/.

All presented shortcuts come from the Visual Studio keyboard scheme.

Write smarter code

The following table contains shortcuts that helps you write the code:

Shortcut	Purpose
Alt + Enter	Displays quick fixes and context actions
Ctrl + R, V	Introduces variable
Alt + Insert	Generates code
Ctrl + E, U	**Surrounds with...**
Ctrl + Space bar	IntelliSense
Ctrl + Alt + Space bar	Smart IntelliSense
Ctrl + W	Extends code selection
Alt + Delete	Safely deletes

Shortcut	Purpose
Ctrl + Shift + F1	Quick documentation
Ctrl + E, L	Live templates
Ctrl + Alt + Insert	File template
Ctrl + R, R	Renames
Ctrl + R, O	Moves to a separate file
Ctrl + Shift + R	**Refactor this...**
Ctrl + D	Duplicate line

Finding what you need quickly

In *Chapter 3, Finding What You Need Quickly*, we have presented you with features that help you find things in a quicker manner. The following table contains shortcuts related to these features:

Shortcut	Purpose
Ctrl + Shift + T	Go to file
Ctrl + T, T	Go to the type
Ctrl + ,	Recent files
Shift + Alt + L	Select file in Solution Explorer
Ctrl + Shift + any number from the keypad	Create a bookmark
Ctrl + same number used to create bookmark	Go to the bookmark
Ctrl + `	List of all bookmarks
Ctrl + Shift + Backspace	Go to the last edited location
Ctrl + T	Go to everything
F12	Go to declaration
Shift + F12	Find usages
Alt + `	Navigate to…
*Alt + *	File members
Ctrl + Alt + F	**File Structure** window
Ctrl + Shift + Alt + A	Value origin and destination

Extended support for web developers

In the chapter related to web development, we introduced only one shortcut, but a very useful one. You can find it in the following table:

Shortcut	Purpose
Ctrl + Alt + F7	Related files

Unit testing

In the following table, you will find shortcuts that will help you run Unit tests:

Shortcut	Purpose
Ctrl + Alt + U	**Unit Test Explorer**
Ctrl + Alt + T	**Unit Test Sessions**
Ctrl + U, L	Run all unit tests in a solution
Ctrl + U, Y	Run unit tests from the current session

Index

Thank you for buying
ReSharper Essentials

About Packt Publishing

Packt, pronounced 'packed', published its first book *"Mastering phpMyAdmin for Effective MySQL Management"* in April 2004 and subsequently continued to specialize in publishing highly focused books on specific technologies and solutions.

Our books and publications share the experiences of your fellow IT professionals in adapting and customizing today's systems, applications, and frameworks. Our solution based books give you the knowledge and power to customize the software and technologies you're using to get the job done. Packt books are more specific and less general than the IT books you have seen in the past. Our unique business model allows us to bring you more focused information, giving you more of what you need to know, and less of what you don't.

Packt is a modern, yet unique publishing company, which focuses on producing quality, cutting-edge books for communities of developers, administrators, and newbies alike. For more information, please visit our website: www.packtpub.com.

Writing for Packt

We welcome all inquiries from people who are interested in authoring. Book proposals should be sent to author@packtpub.com. If your book idea is still at an early stage and you would like to discuss it first before writing a formal book proposal, contact us; one of our commissioning editors will get in touch with you.

We're not just looking for published authors; if you have strong technical skills but no writing experience, our experienced editors can help you develop a writing career, or simply get some additional reward for your expertise.

Visual Studio 2012 and .NET 4.5 Expert Development Cookbook

ISBN: 978-1-84968-670-9   Paperback: 380 pages

Over 40 recipes for successfully mixing the powerful capabilities of .NET 4.5 and Visual Studio 2012

1. Step-by-step instructions to learn the power of .NET development with Visual Studio 2012

2. Filled with examples that clearly illustrate how to integrate with the technologies and frameworks of your choice

3. Each sample demonstrates key concepts to build your knowledge of the architecture in a practical and incremental way

C++ Application Development with Code::Blocks

ISBN: 978-1-78328-341-5   Paperback: 128 pages

Develop advanced applications with Code::Blocks quickly and efficiently with this concise, hands-on guide

1. Successfully install and configure Code::Blocks for C++ development

2. Perform rapid application development with Code::Blocks

3. Work with advanced C++ features including code debugging and GUI toolkits

Please check **www.PacktPub.com** for information on our titles

Reporting with Visual Studio and Crystal Reports

ISBN: 978-1-78217-802-6   Paperback: 148 pages

Create a reporting application from scratch using Visual Studio and Crystal Reports

1. A step-by-step guide that goes beyond theory, letting you get hands-on experience

2. Utilize a dataset and table adapter as data sources for your report

3. Learn how to add reports to forms and pass parameters dynamically

---

Software Testing using Visual Studio 2012

ISBN: 978-1-84968-954-0   Paperback: 444 pages

Learn different testing techniques and features of Visual Studio 2012 with detailed explanations and real-time samples

1. Using Test Manager and managing test cases and test scenarios

2. Exploratory testing using Visual Studio 2012

3. Learn unit testing features and coded user interface testing

4. Advancement in web performance testing and recording of user scenarios

Please check **www.PacktPub.com** for information on our titles